NNOVATORS

STORIES BEHIND THE PEOPLE WHO SHAPED THE WORLD

25 PROJECTS

MARCIA AMIDON LUSTED

Illustrated by Tom Casteel

~ More science titles in the *Build It Yourself* series ~

Check out more titles at www.nomadpress.net

Nomad Press
A division of Nomad Communications
10 9 8 7 6 5 4 3 2 1

This book was manufactured by Marquis Book Printing,
Montmagny, Québec, Canada
July 2017, Job #136267
ISBN Softcover: 978-1-61930-520-5
ISBN Hardcover: 978-1-61930-516-8

Educational Consultant, Marla Conn

Questions regarding the ordering of this book should be addressed to
Nomad Press
2456 Christian St.
White River Junction, VT 05001
www.nomadpress.net

Printed in Canada.

CONTENTS

PS

Interested in Primary Sources?

Look for this icon. Use a smartphone or tablet app to scan the QR code and explore more. You can find a list of URLs on the Resources page.

If the QR code doesn't work, try searching the Internet with the Keyword Prompts to find other helpful sources.

innovators 🔎

236 BCE: Archimedes designs the first working elevator.

1440: Johannes Gutenberg invents the printing press.

1769: James Watt invents the steam engine.

1789: Benjamin Banneker successfully predicts a solar eclipse.

1794: Eli Whitney patents the cotton gin.

1796: Dr. Edward Jenner develops a vaccine to inoculate against smallpox.

1811: Mary Anning finds the skeleton of an ichthyosaur in Lime Regis, England.

1839: Eliza Lucas Pinckney begins working to improve the indigo plant.

1844: Samuel Morse invents Morse Code to use with the telegraph machine.

1928: Alexander Fleming discovers penicillin.

1927: Philo T. Farnsworth demonstrates the first working television.

1930: Ruth Wakefield invents the chocolate chip cookie.

1941: The codebreakers of Bletchley Park break the Enigma machine code.

1943: Richard James invents the Slinky.

1945: Percy Spencer invents the microwave oven.

1947: Ole Kirk Christiansen invents the Lego building brick.

1948: Maria Telkes and Eleanor Raymond design a solar home.

1950: George Lerner invents Mr. Potato Head.

1995: Jeff Bezos starts the online retail site Amazon.com.

1997: Sergey Brin and Larry Page start Google.

2003: Skype is invented.

2006: Twitter is invented.

iv

1923: Garrett Morgan invents the traffic light.

1926: Robert Goddard tests the first liquid-fueled rocket.

1905: Madam C.J. Walker launches her beauty business.

1900: Mary Anderson invents the windshield wiper.

1991: Dr. Ann Tsukamoto helps create a process for isolating stem cells to fight cancer.

1981: Dr. Patricia Bath invents a new laser treatment for cataracts.

1893: Dr. Daniel Hale Williams performs the first open-heart surgery.

1978: Ben Cohen and Jerry Greenfield start Ben & Jerry's Ice Cream.

1890: John Froehlich invents the tractor.

2016: Pokémon Go! is released, invented by John Hanke.

2013: Elon Musk releases plans for the Hyperloop transportation system.

1966: Stephanie Kwolek invents the fabric Kevlar.

1886: Ottmar Mergenthaler invents the linotype machine.

1868: Margaret Knight invents a machine to make flat-bottomed paper bags.

1962: Rachel Carson publishes her book, *Silent Spring*.

1952: Dr. Virginia Apgar creates the Apgar test for newborns.

1964: Douglas Engelbart invents the computer mouse.

1862: Dr. Louis Pasteur develops his theory of fermentation and bacteria.

1852: Elisha Otis invents the safety elevator.

1847: Maria Mitchell discovers a comet, which is named after her.

1853: George Crum invents the potato chip.

1857: Joseph Gayetty invents toilet paper.

v

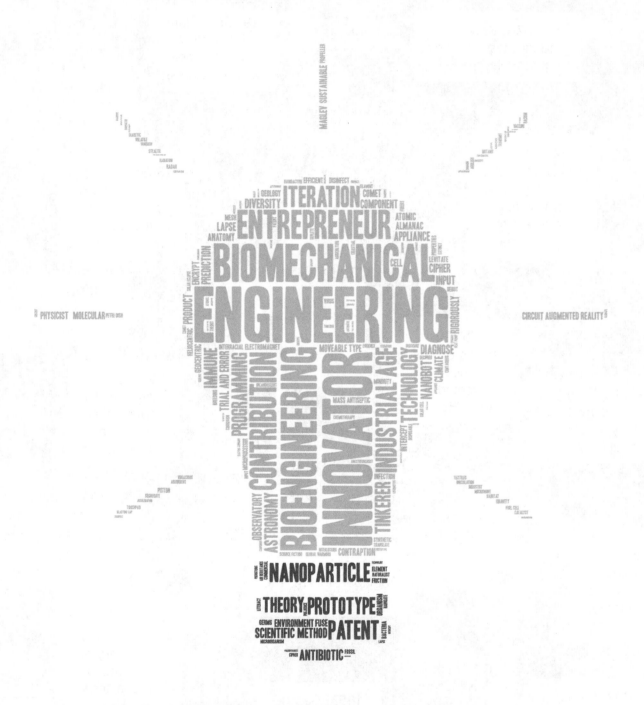

INVENTORS AND INNOVATORS

Henry Ford and his Model T car. Stephanie Kwolek and Kevlar. Thomas Edison and the phonograph. Ruth Wakefield and chocolate chip cookies. The Wright brothers and the airplane. Can you name other famous inventors and their inventions?

An inventor is someone who makes or creates something new to address a particular need. For example, the invention of the telegraph helped connect people separated by great distances in a growing and changing world. Some inventions, however, are happy accidents—like the Slinky or Silly Putty!

The earliest inventions were tools of survival, such as the wheel and the arrow. Later inventions include the printing press, telephone, steam engine, camera, and sewing machine. Can you image life without modern inventions such as the television, computer, and cell phone?

innovator: a person who introduces new methods, ideas, or products.

spear: a weapon with a long shaft and pointed tip, used for thrusting or throwing.

technology: tools, methods, and systems used to solve a problem or do work.

diversity: when many different people or things exist within a group or place.

contribution: a part played by a person or thing in bringing about a result.

minority: a group of people, such as African Americans, that is smaller than or different from the larger group. Minorities are often subject to discrimination.

product: an item, such as a book or clothing, that is made and sold to people.

industry: a branch of business or employment.

WORDS TO KNOW

For every famous inventor who creates something completely new, there are many other people who take those inventions and make them better. These people are often called **innovators**.

Innovators look at an invention and think about ways to improve it. They work with inventors by taking their ideas a step further. An ancient innovator probably looked at a sharpened rock used as a knife and thought that it would be even more useful attached to a long stick. That innovator made the first **spear**.

Innovators might improve a recent invention or they might look at an invention that has been around for a very long time and make it better using modern technology.

Diversity in Innovation

When you read about inventors and innovators during the course of history, you might notice that many or most of them were white men. Where is the **diversity** in this group of people? Why weren't women and people of color inventors and innovators? Actually, they were innovators, but when a woman or person of color made a discovery, the credit would often go to the person they were working for, who was usually a white man. The **contributions** of women and people in **minority** populations have often been overlooked or forgotten. It's important to remember that people of all colors and both genders have helped create the world we know today.

Inventors and innovators are partners in creating new **products**, devices, and ways of doing things that make our lives easier, better, and healthier. The modern world needs both of them. We need inventors to come up with new ideas, and we need innovators to make those ideas even better and apply them in ways that the inventor might not even have thought about.

Many inventors are innovators and innovators are inventors! There are also people who seem to stick to one role.

DID YOU KNOW?

In *Innovators: The Stories Behind the People Who Shaped the World*, you'll explore some of the inventors and innovators who have made huge contributions to our world. We'll look at many different **industries**, including health, science, technology, food, and even toys!

Each chapter of this book begins with an essential question to help guide your exploration of inventors and innovators. Keep the question in your mind as you read the chapter. At the end of each chapter, use your engineering notebook to record your thoughts and answers.

We'll meet innovators who used their knowledge and imaginations to take inventions in different areas even further. We'll be looking at some inventors who have changed our lives and yet aren't very well known. We'll also meet innovators whose work improves lives every single day.

Did you know that some of these innovators and inventors are not much older than you? By exploring their work through activities and projects, you might be inspired to become one of the next generation of people whose ideas can change the world!

ESSENTIAL QUESTION

What is the difference between inventors and innovators?

Engineering Design Process

Every **engineer** and innovator keeps a notebook to keep track of their ideas and their steps in the engineering design process. As you read through this book and do the activities, keep track of your observations, data, and designs in an engineering design worksheet, like the one shown here. When doing an activity, remember that there is no right answer or right way to approach a project. Be creative and have fun!

Problem: What problem are we trying to solve?

Research: Has anything been invented to help solve the problem? What can we learn?

Question: Are there any special requirements for the device? An example of this is a car that must go a certain distance in a certain amount of time.

Brainstorm: Draw lots of designs for your device and list the materials you are using!

Prototype: Build the design you drew during brainstorming.

Test: Test your **prototype** and record your observations.

Evaluate: Analyze your test results. Do you need to make adjustments? Do you need to try a different prototype?

Through the Years

Some of the inventions we use today existed long ago, but in completely different forms. The telephone that Alexander Graham Bell patented in 1876, for example, looks much different from the smartphone you might carry in your pocket today. In this activity, you will research a product and create a timeline showing the development of that product from its earliest iteration to its current form.

Think of an invention that has been around for several decades. Some ideas include the telephone, the computer, the bicycle, and the car.

Research the history of this product. Find out important facts about it.

* Who invented it?

* What did it first look like?

* What problem did it solve?

* How did it fail before it succeeded?

* How many people contributed to its success?

* How has it changed during its lifespan?

* What does it look like now?

* How is that different from what it looked like earlier?

Record your research and create a timeline in your engineering design notebook. How do you think this invention will change in the future? What modifications would you make to improve it? Include your redesigned product of the future in your timeline.

THINK MORE: Think about the market for your future product. Who will want it and how will they use it? How much will it cost? How will you promote your product? Create a marketing campaign that entices people to buy it.

WORDS TO KNOW

patent: a right given to only one inventor to manufacture, use, or sell an invention for a certain number of years.

iteration: the repetition of a process in order to make a product better and better.

ACTIVITY

5

Chapter 1

THE MEDICAL WORLD

How do you feel about being given a shot at the doctor's office? Have you taken medicine to fight an **infection** or know someone who has had a blood transfusion? Inventors and innovators helped make all those things possible!

Have you ever heard of typhoid, polio, or smallpox? Although you might not know what they are, in the eighteenth and nineteenth centuries, these diseases terrified people around the world. Highly **contagious** and often deadly, these illnesses killed and **disfigured** millions of people.

? ESSENTIAL QUESTION

How do recent medical discoveries build upon work done in the past?

At the time, doctors and scientists weren't sure what caused these diseases. They didn't know how to prevent their spread. But at the end of the eighteenth century, a pioneering doctor named Edward Jenner (1749–1823) took the first step in developing a **vaccine** to safely prevent and eventually **vanquish** one of the deadliest diseases in history—smallpox.

FIGHTING DISEASE

Named for the small, disfiguring pockmark scars that covered its victims' bodies, smallpox was once a deadly disease without a cure. Nearly one-third of people who contracted the disease died. Those who survived were left covered in scars.

At the time, doctors practiced a kind of **inoculation** called variolation. A small amount of material from the scab of a person infected with smallpox was placed into a cut made on the arm or leg of healthy person. By exposing someone healthy to smallpox, doctors could sometimes keep them from developing the full disease.

However, the risky procedure often backfired. Some patients caught the disease anyway. This spread it further and discouraged others from trying the procedure. It was far from a good way to prevent the disease.

infection: when microorganisms invade and make you sick.

contagious: easy to catch.

disfigure: to spoil the looks of something.

vaccine: medicine designed to keep a person from getting a particular disease, usually given by needle.

vanquish: to thoroughly defeat.

inoculation: a shot or medicine given to people to protect them from a certain disease or illness.

devastating: highly destructive or damaging.

WORDS TO KNOW

Polio is a **devastating** disease that affects the body's muscles. Before the vaccine for polio was invented, many children got polio. Some could no longer walk and some needed machines to breathe for them.

DID YOU KNOW?

7

pus: a thick yellowish or greenish liquid produced by an infection.

incision: an opening made in the skin.

immune: the ability of a person to resist a disease or illness.

vaccination: another word for inoculation.

germs: microorganisms that causes diseases.

organism: a living thing.

theory: an unproven idea used to explain something.

microorganism: a living thing that is so small it can be seen only with a microscope. Also called a microbe.

spontaneous generation: an idea, known now to be not true, that life comes from something non-living.

WORDS TO KNOW

In 1796, the English physician Edward Jenner discovered a much safer and more effective way to protect people from the deadly contagion—with the help of cows. Having grown up in a small town in the English countryside, Jenner often heard stories of farmhands protected from smallpox after catching cowpox. This is a similar but non-fatal disease people could catch from cows.

After investigating these tales, Jenner became convinced that exposure to the mild cowpox could prevent someone from catching and spreading the deadly smallpox. He placed a small amount of **pus** from a cowpox sore into a small **incision** in the arm of an eight-year-old boy, and quickly proved that he was **immune** to smallpox.

Medical experts of the time rejected his idea, but Jenner continued his experiments. Two years after his first experiment, Jenner's innovative approach to fighting disease was accepted by the medical community, and the practice spread around the world. Jenner called his technique **vaccination**, after the Latin word *vacca* for "cow." In 1980, the World Health Organization declared that smallpox was eliminated around the world—thanks to Edward Jenner and a few cows.

Doctors still didn't know exactly what caused people to get smallpox in the first place. It wasn't until a few decades later that a scientist suspected it was something very small.

Defense Against Disease

Vaccines work by giving the body's immune system a crash-course in how to fight a particular disease. A dead or weakened form of the disease is used to help the body recognize it and fight off the real illness. Today, vaccines are a common way to fight many diseases, including measles, mumps, and whooping cough. Do you get vaccinations at the doctor's office? What do you think modern society would be like if we didn't have the power of vaccinations to protect us from many diseases?

IT'S THE LITTLE THINGS

Most of us learn about **germs** from the time we're very young. We're taught to wash our hands and not to cough or sneeze on other people. But the idea of germs didn't exist before the ground-breaking work of a French chemist named Louis Pasteur (1822–1895).

Early in his career, Pasteur was contacted by a man whose factory made beer out of sugar beets. The vats of beer kept going sour, and the frustrated owner did not know why.

When Pasteur looked at the liquid under a microscope, he discovered thousands of tiny organisms.

Pasteur developed the **theory** that these **microorganisms** were causing the beer to go bad. But where did these little things come from? For thousands of years, people had believed in **spontaneous generation**. People thought that corn turned into mice and rotting meat turned into maggots! That might seem silly to us now, but back then, this was the most popular theory.

INNOVATORS

nutrient: a substance an organism needs to live and grow.

virus: a small infectious microbe.

bacteria: microorganisms found in soil, water, plants, and animals that are sometimes harmful.

disinfect: to clean something in order to destroy bacteria.

antiseptic: a substance that prevents the growth of disease-causing microorganisms.

antibiotic: a medicine that destroys microorganisms that cause illness or infection.

WORDS TO KNOW

After discovering these tiny living creatures, Pasteur had an idea. Perhaps food rotted thanks to the presence of microorganisms.

To test his hypothesis, Pasteur performed an experiment that changed science forever.

Pasteur placed a **nutrient** broth—kind of like soup—into two glass containers. One container had a straight neck, like a soda straw, sticking straight up and open to the air. The other had a curved neck, like a bendable straw, also open to the air. He brought both containers of broth to a boil, and then let them cool.

For many days, Pasteur observed the containers. The broth in the container with the straight neck became cloudy and dark, while the broth in the container with the curved neck didn't change.

10

Pasteur correctly realized that tiny microorganisms could easily fall from the air into the container with the straight neck. The curved neck of the other container prevented the microorganisms from reaching the broth.

By disproving spontaneous generation, Pasteur set the stage for the realization that microorganisms, including **viruses** and **bacteria**, could do more than spoil meat and beer. Microorganisms could be a source of disease.

WASH YOUR HANDS!

Have you seen surgeons on TV "scrub in" before operating? Do you wash your hands before you eat or if you get a cut?

The work of Joseph Lister (1827–1912) built on Pasteur's discovery of germs. Lister realized that many people in hospitals often survived surgery, but later died from infections. He noticed that doctors in these hospitals were moving from patient to patient, from surgery to surgery, without washing their hands or even their instruments!

Today, we know to wash our hands whenever germs might be present. In the nineteenth century, it was a radical idea that changed medicine and our lives forever.

DID YOU KNOW?

Lister understood that patients' wounds became infected because microorganisms were getting into them. He taught doctors to **disinfect** their hands and also pioneered the use of **antiseptic** bandages and treatments.

The discovery of microorganisms and how to prevent their spread was advanced even further with the discovery of the first antibiotics.

WORDS TO KNOW

mold: a furry growth.

petri dish: a circular, flat, transparent dish for growing microorganisms.

organic: something that is or was living.

bacterium: a single bacteria.

interracial: existing between or involving different races of people.

transfusion: the process of transferring blood into a human's circulatory system.

cell: the most basic part of a living thing.

reconstitute: to restore something dried to its original state by adding water.

segregate: to keep apart.

In 1928, a doctor named Alexander Fleming (1881–1955) returned to his laboratory after a vacation to find a messy and cluttered desk. While cleaning up, he noticed **mold** had grown in some of his **petri dishes**. Mold grows in moist warm conditions, especially on food or other **organic** matter. The petri dishes contained a common **bacterium** he'd been researching. Curious, he placed the dishes under a microscope and was surprised to see that the mold had stopped the bacteria from growing.

Fleming had discovered penicillin, a life-saving antibiotic used to treat infections.

During World War II, scientists learned to make large amounts of penicillin to treat soldiers' wounds and illnesses. Today, your doctor might give you penicillin to help your body fight off a bacterial infection.

The discovery of microorganisms and how to guard against them during and after surgery allowed surgeons to attempt more difficult and daring operations. These included trying to fix a beating heart!

CLOSE TO THE HEART

In 1891, Dr. Daniel Hale Williams (1856–1931), a surgeon working in Chicago, Illinois, opened the city's first **interracial** hospital. Williams became one of the first African-American doctors in the city.

Good News for Vampires

Another innovator in the medical field was Dr. Charles Drew (1904–1950). He was a surgeon in Washington, DC, who studied blood **transfusions**. There was no good way to store blood for use during emergencies, and he began to work on a method for processing and preserving blood plasma, which is blood without **cells**. Plasma lasts much longer than the whole blood that we have in our veins, and could be stored, or banked, for long periods of time.

Drew's discovery made it possible for hospitals to create blood banks to store blood for future use. He also found that plasma could be dried and then **reconstituted** when a patient needed it. Drew was an African American. Ironically, he found himself acting as head of a program that collected and shipped blood overseas but **segregated** the blood of black people from the blood of white people.

Williams' biggest contribution to medicine was performing the first open-heart surgery.

In the 1890s, most wounds to the heart were considered fatal. But when a man with a stab wound to the chest arrived at his hospital, Williams successfully repaired the lining of the heart. It was the first open-heart surgery. Thanks to an understanding of germs and sanitary practices, Williams paved the way for today's amazing surgeons.

YOUR FIRST TEST!

Not all medical innovations have had to do with disease and injury—some of the most important medical practices happen as soon as we're born. Dr. Virginia Apgar (1909–1974) was the first woman at Columbia University College of Physicians and Surgeons to become a full professor. An **anesthesiologist**, Apgar began studying the effects of using anesthesia on mothers giving birth.

In the 1940s, delivery-room doctors focused most of their attention on mothers. There wasn't much they could do to help a sick or weak newborn, they thought. But Apgar wondered if more could be done for children immediately after birth.

She realized that there needed to be a way to evaluate the health of babies just moments after they were born. Doctors needed to see how the babies were affected by the anesthesia.

Apgar developed a test that examined five specific aspects of a baby's health: heart rate, breathing, muscle tone, reflexes, and color.

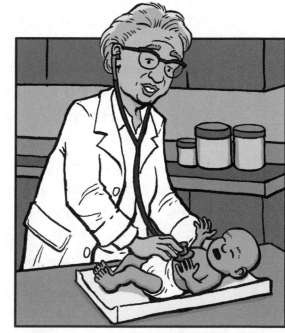

Each aspect is given a score, between 0 and 2 points, and the total is the baby's Apgar score. This system allows doctors and nurses to quickly evaluate a baby's health and take any necessary actions to help it. Apgar is credited with saving the lives of thousands of newborns, and her test is still used today with every baby born in a hospital.

MODERN MARVELS

Medical innovations don't live exclusively in the past. In fact, almost every day brings news of new discoveries and treatments. Scientists work off the inventions of the past to create a healthier future. Many doctors and scientists are researching new ways to treat and maybe even cure cancer, which kills 7.4 million people every year. And it's not just scientists who are working on the problem.

In 2012, while he was still in high school, Jack Andraka (1997–) might have invented a new way to detect pancreatic cancer in its early stages.

He created a sensor that is similar to the test strips used by **diabetics** to test their blood. Andraka is trying to create a test that is faster, less expensive, and more accurate than other tests. His discovery has long years of testing ahead of it.

For his work so far, Andraka won the grand prize at the Intel International Science and Engineering Fair. He is currently attending Stanford University in California, studying **bioengineering**. Andraka's studies focus on **nanobots** that can destroy cancer cells.

Angela Zhang (1995–) is another young innovator who is working to fight cancer. She is a student at Harvard University who is studying **biomechanical engineering**.

nanoparticle: a microscopic particle of matter.

chemotherapy: a treatment for cancer that uses chemicals.

atomic: having to do with atoms, the tiny particles of matter that make up everything.

molecular: having to do with molecules, the groups of atoms bound together to form everything.

insulin: a hormone in the body that regulates sugar in the blood.

diagnose: to find and identify a problem.

WORDS TO KNOW

At the age of 17, Zhang gave President Barack Obama a science lesson about her cancer-fighting nanoparticles at a White House science fair.

Zhang was part of a research team at Stanford University. The team was developing an iron oxide gold nanoparticle that can both detect cancer and deliver **chemotherapy** drugs directly to the cells that need it. In college, she has teamed up with other Harvard students to establish a nonprofit group that provides used laboratory equipment to American high schools that can't afford to buy it.

Much of the ongoing research into cancer prevention and treatment is based on the work of a scientist named Dr. Ann Tsukamoto (1952–). In 1991, she co-patented the process used to isolate the human stem cell. Stem cells are different from other types of cells because they are not specialized in the way that muscle cells, lung cells, or skin cells are.

Nanotechnology

Nanotechnology is the science of working with extremely small materials, so small that they can be measured only on an **atomic**, or **molecular**, scale. Think of objects the size of $1/800$ the thickness of a human hair. These materials are often used to build tiny robots that could be used to attack cancer cells in the human bloodstream or repair damage to cells themselves. You can see gold nanoparticles forming chains in the video on this website.

Argonne gold nanoparticles 🔍

Stem cells can renew themselves during a long period of time. They also can be made to take on the functions of other specialized cells, such as those that produce **insulin** in the body or make the heart beat. Stem cells are vital to cancer research because understanding how they grow and reproduce has helped researchers better understand how cancer cells work.

Tsukamoto's work with stem cells allowed other scientists to make strides in fighting this terrible disease.

Medical discoveries never stand alone. Each innovation is a building block from the past into the future, and all of them together create a bigger base for the scientific discoveries that are still to come. Every new piece of knowledge leads innovators in medicine to better ways of preventing, **diagnosing**, and treating diseases, conditions, and injuries. The more we think, the healthier we can be.

?

ESSENTIAL QUESTION

Now it's time to consider and discuss the Essential Question: How do recent medical discoveries build upon work done in the past?

17

Wash Your Hands

How easy is it to spread germs? Find out by experimenting with handwashing times! We can't see the germs on your hands, so you need to find something to put on your hands that acts like germs.

Think about how you want to simulate germs on your hands. Come up with a plan to clean the substance off your hands. Create an engineering design worksheet in your notebook with the problem you are trying to solve and possible solutions. Design a method of keeping track of how dirty your hands are—maybe you'll use a number between one and 10 to record the dirt level. Create a chart to keep track of your observations.

Spread some of the "germs" on your hands. Spread it evenly over both hands, including the backs of the hands and the skin next to and under the fingernails. How dirty can you get your hands? Record the dirt level using your system.

Wash your hands for a short amount of time, record the results, then wash again for a longer time, and record those results. Keep washing and recording your results until your hands are as clean as they can be!

Present your results in a graph. What conclusions can you draw from your data? How does the length of the handwashing affect the cleanliness of the hands and the amount of "germs"?

THINK MORE: How does the spread of germs affect people around you? Think about all the surfaces you touch in your home or classroom. Can you create an experiment, based on the activity you just did, that shows how germs spread from person to person and how far they can travel through contact? Can you come up with some ways to prevent spreading the germs that can cause illness?

What's in Your Blood?

Scientists often use models to help them visualize the discoveries they are trying to make. In this project, you'll make a model of the components of blood to better visualize cures for the diseases that affect the blood.

Blood is not just one single thing, but a combination of four. What are the four components that make up blood?

* plasma
* red blood cells
* white blood cells
* platelets

Research the percentage of each component in our blood. How much of each component is within each measure of blood? What does each material do? How do they interact with each other?

Decide on materials to use to represent each of the four components of blood. Can you find ingredients that match in size? What sort of container will you use to hold all of your components?

Research diseases in which the normal composition of blood is changed. How do the percentages change? Using the same materials, create models for blood percentages for several diseases, such as leukemia. What do you learn about the behavior of blood under these types of stress?

THINK MORE: Not everyone has the same type of blood. Research the common types of blood, and the role of RH. Does the composition of blood change depending on what blood type that person has? Does it change depending on the blood's RH factor? Can you create models for the different blood types? How do they compare? Are there differences?

WORDS TO KNOW

component: a part or piece of a larger whole, especially of a machine or a vehicle.

Chapter 2

SOLVING PROBLEMS WITH SCIENCE

As long as humans have been around, they have wondered about the world. Why is the world the way it is? How can we explore it and what can we learn about it? Some innovators have focused on the earth, while others have looked at the skies above. Inventors and innovators have found ways of traveling farther and farther and discovering more about the planet and the space around us.

Do you want to be a scientist? From **astronomy** to **zoology**, the innovative ideas of scientists have led to some of the most important discoveries in history. Today's researchers build on the innovations and insights of the past, looking for new and exciting ways to help us explore and learn about the world.

ESSENTIAL QUESTION

How does studying the natural world spark ideas for improvements in technology?

A TOWER AND A TELESCOPE

Galileo Galilee (1564–1642) was born into a wealthy family in Pisa, Italy. Although he went to school to become a physician, Galileo was fascinated with **physics** and mathematics and devoted most of his studies to these subjects. Always eager to take a new look at long-held beliefs, Galileo performed a simple **gravity** experiment that started him on a career that would change the world.

astronomy: the scientific study of the stars and planets.

zoology: the study of animals.

physics: the study of physical forces, including matter, energy, and motion, and how these forces interact with each other.

gravity: a force that pulls all objects toward the earth.

air resistance: the force of air pushing against an object.

mass: the amount of material that an object contains.

acceleration: the process of increasing the speed of an object's movement.

sphere: a round object, such as a ball.

WORDS TO KNOW

If you drop a sheet of paper and a book at the same time, which will hit the ground first? During Galileo's time, scientists believed that the heavier an object was, the faster it fell. But Galileo's own experience told him otherwise. He believed that it was **air resistance**, not a difference in **mass**, that caused objects to fall at different rates.

To determine if an object's **acceleration** depended on its mass, he dropped two heavy **spheres** of different weights from the famous Leaning Tower of Pisa. He found that the mass of the spheres didn't matter—they both reached the ground at nearly the same time. He also concluded that if two objects fall at different rates, it's due to air resistance. Without air, even a feather and a hammer would fall at the same rate!

Galileo's experiment was a simple and innovative way to overturn centuries of scientific thinking.

scientific method: the way scientists ask questions and do experiments to try to prove their ideas.

rigorously: in an extremely thorough and careful way.

evidence: the available facts or information supporting or denying a theory.

geocentric: a model of the universe, now disproved, that the earth is the center of the solar system.

heliocentric: a model of the universe in which the planets orbit the sun and the moon orbits the earth.

excommunicate: to officially exclude someone from participating in the sacraments and religious services of the Christian Church.

WORDS TO KNOW

Galileo is sometimes called the "father of the **scientific method**." While he didn't invent the process, he was one of the first scientists to **rigorously** use observation and experimentation to explore the world. His **evidence**-based approach helped him greatly when news of a fantastic new invention reached Italy.

In 1609, after learning of the creation of a spyglass that allowed people to see across great distances, Galileo built his own version and pointed it at the sky. At the time, most scientists believed that the earth was the center of the universe, and everything else revolved around it.

This **geocentric** model had been challenged by Nicolaus Copernicus a century earlier. Still, his **heliocentric**, or sun-centered, view was shunned by the powerful Catholic Church.

Testing Gravity on the Moon

It can be hard to find the right conditions under which to test Galileo's theory of gravity. Where can you find a place with no air? How about the moon? Watch *Apollo 15* astronaut David Scott perform Galileo's experiment on the moon, where there isn't any air to provide air resistance. Scott used a feather and a hammer!

Apollo 15 hammer feather 🔍

Pointing the Finger

Almost 100 years after Galileo died, someone snapped his middle finger off! After being passed around for a couple hundred years, the finger ended up in the History of Science Museum in Florence, Italy, where it was joined by two more of Galileo's fingers and a tooth. The middle finger is kept in a glass dome and points up toward the sky.

But what Galileo saw through his telescope was the beginning of the end for geocentrism.

Galileo discovered the moon to be covered in deep craters and towering mountains—far from the perfectly flat disk that was the accepted view of the Church! He also discovered that Venus's changing brightness is due to phases, just like the moon. And even more surprising to the Italian was that Jupiter is surrounded by four small "stars" that circle the world in patterns much like those of the planets.

Galileo's observations provided proof that Earth is not the center of the solar system. But his views came at a cost. Although the Church funded much of Galileo's work, the idea of an imperfect, sun-centered universe was too much. Galileo was **excommunicated**, forced from the Church for his work and beliefs.

Galileo's determination and rigorous scientific explorations helped shape the world we see today. But Galileo isn't alone. There are many others whose hard work and curiosity in the face of obstacles changed the world around them.

Although his findings ultimately proved true and were accepted, it wasn't until 1992 that the Church officially apologized for its treatment of Galileo.

DID YOU KNOW?

23

THE SELF-TAUGHT TINKERER

Benjamin Banneker (1731–1806) was one of these curious people. The son of a former slave and a free woman, Banneker was born long before slavery was **abolished**. Banneker had little formal schooling and learned to read from his grandmother. Growing up near Baltimore, Maryland, he taught himself astronomy, mathematics, engineering, and anything else that caught his interest.

When he was just 15, he designed an **irrigation** system for his family's farm that kept it thriving even during **droughts**. A **tinkerer**, he would often take apart and reassemble machinery—including a friend's watch!—just to see how it worked. His inquisitive nature and fondness for mathematics soon led him to some amazing accomplishments.

But Banneker wasn't interested only in small machines. When he gazed at the night sky, he saw more than just stars and planets. He saw their motions as patterns that could be used to make calculations and **predictions**. In 1789, his extensive research in astronomy and mathematics led to the accurate prediction and description of a **solar eclipse**.

Banneker used his knowledge of engineering and mathematics to build the first striking clock made in America. Made entirely out of pieces of carved wood, it kept accurate time for decades.

DID YOU KNOW?

24

Banneker's Almanack

Banneker used his astronomical and mathematical knowledge to write and publish **almanacs**. These contained predictions of astronomical occurrences and eclipses, high tides, and even the likelihood of locust swarms. The data helped fishermen, farmers, and even the military to be more productive and efficient in their work. You can see Banneker's almanacs on the Smithsonian Institution's website.

Benjamin Banneker's Almanack 🔍

His calculations went against those of several famous and professional astronomers, but Banneker's proved to be the most accurate.

Benjamin Banneker was also an outspoken critic of slavery. He wrote to President Thomas Jefferson to persuade him that the quest for freedom from Britain should also include freedom for slaves. Jefferson was impressed with Banneker's many accomplishments. He insisted that Banneker join the team that was designing the layout of Washington, DC, the new nation's capital.

When the lead designer for the new city quit and took his plans with him, Banneker was able to re-create them in incredible detail. Thanks to his skills as an engineer and his attention to detail, Washington, DC, grew to become the city it is today.

Banneker was one of the first African Americans to distinguish himself in science, despite widespread **prejudice** and **racism**. Bold, curious, and self-educated, he never hesitated to forge his own path in science, engineering, and human rights.

BEAUTY AND POETRY

Another person who flourished in the face of prejudice was Maria Mitchell (1818–1889). She was America's first acknowledged female astronomer at a time when women were often discouraged and even barred from pursuing careers in science. Fortunately, Mitchell's father was an astronomer, and he believed that women deserved the same education and opportunities as men.

Mitchell's father taught her about the night sky, the motions of the planets, and the mathematical laws that governed them. She devoured as many books as she could find on the subject and studied the sky every chance she got using a telescope in her father's **observatory**.

Celestial observers such as Mitchell were called "computers," because they were doing work that would help with computing distances for the developing science of weather prediction.

DID YOU KNOW?

Mitchell was especially interested in **comets**, which were poorly understood at the time. She spent many hours scanning the heavens for evidence of a new comet making its way through the solar system—a very long and often boring task.

Mae Jamison in Space

Dr. Mae Jemison (1956–) was a medical doctor, but she never let go of a lifelong dream to become an astronaut. She applied to the National Aeronautics and Space Administration (NASA) astronaut training program and was chosen to start training as a science mission specialist. It was her responsibility to conduct experiments to improve crew health. In 1992, Jemison went into space on the shuttle *Endeavour* and became the first African-American female astronaut. During eight days in space, she did experiments in weightlessness and motion sickness.

But her hard work paid off—on October 1, 1847, Mitchell discovered a comet. It was the first time an American had discovered a comet. It was named "Miss Mitchell's Comet," and, because of her discovery, Mitchell was elected to the American Academy of Arts and Sciences. She would be the only woman admitted to the academy for almost 100 years!

In 1849, the U.S. Coast Guard hired Mitchell as a celestial observer, and she became the first woman to be paid based on her knowledge in an academic field. Her observations helped the Coast Guard and Navy **navigate** by using precise tables of stars and their locations in the sky.

> **"We especially need imagination in science. It is not all mathematics, nor all logic, but is somewhat beauty and poetry."**
> **—Maria Mitchell**

transit: passing through or across.

radiation: energy that comes from a source and travels through something, such as the radiation from an X-ray that travels through a person.

radioactivity: the emission of a stream of particles or electromagnetic rays.

electromagnetic: one of the fundamental forces of the universe that is responsible for magnetic attraction and electrical charges.

element: a substance whose atoms are all the same. Examples include gold, oxygen, nitrogen, and carbon.

radioactive: describes a chemical substance made of a type of atom that changes because its positively charged particles escape from its center over time.

WORDS TO KNOW

In addition to her own studies, Mitchell taught astronomy to women and inspired others to explore their own scientific interests. In 1888, she and her students photographed and studied a rare **transit** of Venus, capturing images of the planet as it passed directly between the sun and the earth. Mitchell's legacy is even honored on the moon, where later astronomers named one of the lunar craters, "Maria Mitchell."

While Maria Mitchell was breaking barriers for women in the United States, a young woman left her home in Eastern Europe to study an interesting phenomenon— **radiation.**

CURIOUS ABOUT RADIOACTIVITY

When most people think about radiation, they imagine superheroes with fantastic powers—or getting X-rays at the dentist. But there's more to radiation than mutants and dental checkups.

Marie Curie (1867–1934) was a Polish-born scientist and researcher fascinated with science. She might be the most famous female scientist of all time. She was the first woman to win the Nobel Prize and the first person to win it twice in two different fields of study. Her innovative study of radiation and **radioactivity** opened up new fields of study in both chemistry and physics.

Born into a family of teachers in Warsaw, Poland, Curie was surrounded by knowledge. A brilliant student at an early age, she attended a university in France because the universities in Poland refused to enroll women. While there, she became captivated by a newly discovered form of **electromagnetic** energy called X-rays. She was curious to see if other things could give off a similar type of invisible energy.

Through her research, she coined the term "radiation." She also discovered two **elements**: radium, named because it was **radioactive**, and polonium, which she named after her country of birth. Curie studied the properties of these strange materials, fascinated by the way they emitted a form of energy that was invisible to the human eye. During World War I, she called for the use of portable X-ray machines on the battlefield, and is credited with saving the lives of many French soldiers.

Curie's research of radioactivity eventually cost her her own life. Years of exposure to radioactive elements without proper protection caused her to develop aplastic anemia, leading to her death in 1934.

DID YOU KNOW?

"Nothing in life is to be feared, it is only to be understood. Now is the time to understand more, so that we may fear less."
—Marie Curie

Curie's discoveries also led to the use of radiation to treat cancer and other diseases, which has saved the lives of tens of thousands of cancer patients around the world. While Marie Curie is still well-known today, there were many more women before her who helped revolutionize different areas of scientific discovery—including the study of ancient creatures.

WORDS TO KNOW

Jurassic: a period of time that took place from 190 to 140 million years ago.

geology: the study of the earth and its rocks. A scientist who studies geology is a geologist.

fossil: the remains or traces of ancient plants or animals left in rock.

voracious: wanting or devouring great quantities of something.

paleontologist: a scientist who studies fossils.

anatomy: the branch of science having to do with the body structure of living beings.

prehistoric: having to do with ancient times, before written human records.

extinct: when a group of plants or animals dies out and there are no more left in the world.

UNEARTHING THE LIZARDS

Have you heard this tongue twister before? It is based on Mary Anning (1799–1847), who lived in Lyme Regis, England, in the early 1800s.

She sells seashells on the seashore
The shells she sells are seashells, I'm sure
So if she sells seashells on the seashore
Then I'm sure she sells seashore shells.

Lyme Regis is part of what's now called the **Jurassic** Coast, an area full of Earth's ancient history. Recorded in the rocks and cliffs are nearly 185 million years of **geology**, chemistry—and **fossils**. But before they were called fossils, these ancient remains were curiosities for people as well as scientists, including a young Mary Anning.

Anning was born into poverty. To earn extra money for her family, she searched for fossils in the cliffs near her home and sold them to collectors. However, Anning was more than someone who just "sold sea shells." Although she never attended a university, Anning was a **voracious** reader and taught herself everything she could about the strange curiosities she and her family discovered. She became a **paleontologist** known especially for her discoveries of fossils from the Jurassic Period.

In 1833, Mary Anning nearly died in a landslide while searching the cliffs for fossils. The landslide killed her beloved dog.

DID YOU KNOW?

30

Because she was a woman at a time when most scientists were men, Anning was not fully accepted into the scientific community. Most English scientists of the time came from wealthy families in large cities. They were reluctant to acknowledge the work of a woman from a poor, seaside village. She was excluded from many of the societies for geologists and considered a curiosity herself.

However, she became known around the world for her research and people often consulted her on fossils and the **anatomy** of **prehistoric** animals. She learned anatomy so that she could identify the fossils she found and name the parts of the creatures they came from. Every day, she braved unstable cliffs to find fresh fossils, often risking death from landslides, falling rocks, and crashing waves.

Her discoveries included the first full skeleton of an ichthyosaur, an **extinct** reptile resembling a dolphin. Anning helped advance knowledge of prehistoric life by finding connections between living animals and the ancient creatures locked in stone—an approach that was revolutionary. Anning's commitment and passion made her an innovator in her field and an important contributor to scientific knowledge about creatures from the prehistoric world.

Innovations in science don't only help us understand the world around us. Sometimes, innovators use their scientific skills to make money, too.

INDI-GO-GO!

Eliza Lucas Pinckney (1722–1793) was born on the island of Antigua in the West Indies, where her father had a plantation. A strong student and very mature for her age, she was already managing her father's other three plantations near Charleston, South Carolina, by the time she was 16.

climate: the average weather patterns in an area during a long period of time.

botany: the study of plants.

crops: plants grown for food and other uses.

indigo: a tropical plant from the pea family that makes a dark-blue dye.

textiles: having to do with cloth and weaving.

breeding: the development of new types of plants and animals with improved characteristics.

environment: the natural world, especially as it is affected by human activity.

naturalist: an expert in nature and natural history.

marine: having to do with the ocean.

habitat: the natural area where a plant or an animal lives.

pesticide: a chemical used to kill pests on crops.

WORDS TO KNOW

There was a need for new crops that could flourish in the warm **climate** of South Carolina. Pinckney was interested in **botany**, so she decided to see what other **crops** might do well in her new home. One of the plants that she tried was **indigo**. This crop was used to dye **textiles** a deep, rich blue. She was familiar with it because it grew well on her father's Antigua plantation, but the varieties didn't do nearly as well in Charleston.

Pinckney began experimenting with selective **breeding**, choosing strains of indigo that did well. Her plan was to create a variety better suited to growing in South Carolina.

As a result of Pinckney's efforts, indigo exports grew from only 5,000 pounds in 1745 to 130,000 pounds in just three years. Soon, indigo was second only to rice as a moneymaking crop for South Carolina.

Pinckney also experimented with fig trees, hemp, silk, and flax. Although she was not a trained botanist, Pinckney used her love of plants and the science of selective breeding to build a new industry in what would soon become the United States. Today, the process of selective breeding is used around the world to grow stronger, healthier crops that are resistant to disease, drought, and pests. By experimenting, Pinckney helped build a new industry.

Although innovation can lead to scientific advancement and prosperity, there are sometimes unexpected consequences that affect the world in different ways. Many of the things we take for granted, such as clean air and water, were not always a priority. That began to change with the work of Rachel Carson.

PROTECTING THE ENVIRONMENT

While many innovators in science sought to gain knowledge and help others, some saw a need to protect and preserve the **environment** from the harmful effects of industry. A **naturalist** whose work opened people's eyes to these needs was Rachel Carson (1907–1964).

Carson began her work as a **marine** biologist, studying sea creatures and writing books describing their ocean **habitat**. But she also began paying attention to the growing research about the effects of **pesticides** on the environment.

Following World War II, pesticides were used to control unwanted insects on crops, in parks, and in the home. While these pesticides were often successful in getting rid of pests, few considered the negative effects the chemicals were having on wildlife and habitats. In 1962, Carson published a book titled *Silent Spring*, which questioned the direction of modern science.

Was it acceptable to use science without thinking carefully about unintended consequences?

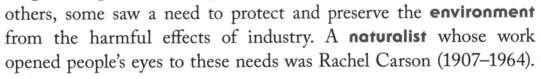

33

She argued that scientists, governments, and society as a whole were responsible for making sure that the world remained a clean, healthy place to live. Carson was an early voice for the environmental movement, and sparked the public's awareness that damage was being done to the natural world. In *Silent Spring*, Carson suggested a new way of thinking about science and nature, and asked if it was acceptable for humans to destroy the natural world.

Because of Carson's book and the questions it raised, President John F. Kennedy launched the first investigation into the effects of pesticides on public health. As a result, dangerous chemicals such as DDT and other harmful pesticides were banned from use, and the foundation was laid for the creation of the Environmental Protection Agency (EPA). Established in 1970, the EPA's purpose is to protect human health and the environment from all types of natural and human-made pollution and contamination. Rachel Carson is sometimes called the "mother of the EPA," and is considered a pioneering innovator in conservation.

When you go outside, what do you like to do? Skateboard, swim, hike, lie in a hammock? Maybe you like to look around and wonder what can you do to help make the environment a healthier place. Will you help extend human knowledge and understanding of our surroundings? Will you be a scientific innovator?

? ESSENTIAL QUESTION

Now it's time to consider and discuss the Essential Question: How does studying the natural world spark ideas for improvements in technology?

How Big Is Our Solar System?

Early astronomers could only estimate the size of the solar system through observation. While today's astronomers have more complex tools for measuring the distances from planet to planet, it's helpful to get a real-life idea of just how vast our solar system is.

Before you begin, write a few paragraphs and draw a sketch showing your own idea of how far apart the planets are from each other and the sun. Don't research this, just sketch your understanding at this time.

Using a long piece of string, decide how to mark the placement of the planets in relation to each other. What can you use to show where each planet is along the string? Once you have decided what marker represents each planet, have them ready to place along the string.

Now, research the placement of the planets in our solar system. Decide how to take the actual distances between them and show them on your long piece of string. Will each thousand miles be one inch? One millimeter? Your system of placing your planets will depend on how long your string is. Do you need a longer string than you first thought?

Once you've created your distance model of the solar system, compare it to your first sketch. How is the model the same as the sketch? How is it different? How has your perception of the size of our solar system changed?

What if the moon were the size of one pixel? Take a look!

moon one pixel 🔍

DID YOU KNOW?

THINK MORE: In addition to showing how far apart the planets are from each other and the sun, can you also show how they compare in size? How can you show that Mercury is smaller than Earth, or that Jupiter is bigger? Does this comparison also change how you thought about the size of the solar system compared to Earth?

Make a Fossil

IDEAS FOR SUPPLIES

large nonabrasive household sponges ☾ wax paper ☾ paraffin wax blocks (2 by 2 by 6 inches) ☾ rubber gloves and safety goggles ☾ tongs

Fossils are remnants of once-living things. One way fossils form is by permineralization. Wood from ancient trees and dinosaur bones were often fossilized by permineralization. This is when the tiny spaces within a bone or piece of wood are filled with mineral-rich water and internal crystals begin to form. Eventually, the whole bone becomes rock. Wood fossilized in this way is called petrified wood.

Caution: Be very careful and have an adult help with heating and melting the wax.

This activity uses a sponge dipped in wax to imitate permineralization. The sponge represents animal bone and the paraffin wax is the permineralizing agent.

Draw or trace the shape of fossils on the sponges and cut the fossil shapes out. Cut a large enough piece of wax paper to hold all the sponge fossils when they are ready to cool.

Place the paraffin blocks in a large pot on high heat. Add just enough water to keep the wax from burning (usually ¼ cup per block of paraffin is enough).

Put on rubber gloves and safety goggles. Have an adult heat the wax to a boil and then lower the heat to minimize hot wax splatters.

WORDS TO KNOW

permineralization: the process of mineral deposits hardening within the tiny spaces of a dead organism.

With an adult's help, use tongs to submerge each sponge fossil for 5 to 10 seconds in the boiling wax. Squish the sponges down with the tongs so that every pore absorbs wax.

Place each sponge fossil onto the wax paper for cooling, being careful not to squeeze the sponge. You don't want any of the wax to be lost from the sponge.

Once it is cool, examine your sponge. What characteristics does it have now? Record your observations in your engineering design notebook.

THINK MORE: Explain in writing or discuss in a group how permineralized fossils form using either the sponge example or one from real life. What will happen to the sponge if it gets hot again or exposed to water? What natural processes can destroy real permineralized fossils?

Citizen Science

Because the science of astronomy involves huge amounts of data, more than what a few computers can handle, it can be easier for scientists to train volunteers to help gather and analyze this data. This is called citizen science, and there are many websites where ordinary people who are interested in astronomy can sign up. One site, SETI@ Home, lets your computer search for extraterrestrial life. Other sites use volunteers to count stars, track solar storms, and map the moon! You can engage in some citizen science at this website.

zooniverse 🔍

Can You See Clearly?

Before electricity, astronomers had an easier time viewing the nighttime sky and seeing stars. Why? Today's astronomers have to deal with light pollution, which is light from streetlights and buildings that lightens the night sky over a large area. You can use observations to determine how much light pollution, as well as factors such as the time of year, the presence of clouds, and the adjustment of your eyes to the dark, affects your viewing of the faintest stars in the sky.

Choose a site where you can observe the constellation Ursa Minor. In your engineering design notebook, write down details about your location, including how much light pollution there is, the sky conditions, weather, and what kind of surroundings there are.

Find a seasonal star chart on the Internet or in a book. You can also download a star chart app. This will tell you what stars are in Ursa Minor. Looking directly into the sky, find Ursa Minor and locate as many of its stars as you can. In your notebook, write down the stars you see and note which are brightest and which are faintest.

Wait 15 minutes, then locate and note the stars again. What differences do you find in your observations of the stars and how bright they are? What happened while you waited?

Do another observation from a location with more light pollution. How does it affect your ability to observe the stars in Ursa Minor? Does your experience change as your eyes adjust to your surroundings? You can also conduct your observation on several different nights when weather conditions are different. Does this change your ability to see the stars?

THINK MORE: How might light pollution affect observatories with huge telescopes? Can you think of other situations or creatures in the natural world that might have been negatively affected by light pollution?

Chapter 3

HAPPIEST AT HOME

There are many inventions and innovations that have to do with technological or medical discoveries. These change human lives on a large scale. But some of the most useful and most practical inventions have to do with small, everyday things that most people don't think twice about.

If you look around your home, you'll find many gadgets, tools, and other products that you use all the time. These things make your life easier—but where did they come from? Who invented them?

? ESSENTIAL QUESTION

What do you think needs improving in your home? Can you think of a device you can invent to improve your own bedroom?

WORDS TO KNOW

trial and error: trying first one thing, then another and another, until something works.

transmit: to broadcast or send out an electrical signal for television or radio.

electric current: the flow of an electrical charge.

fuel cell: something that produces a steady stream of electricity.

solar cell: a device that converts the energy of the sun into electrical energy.

voltage: the force that moves electricity along a wire.

POWERING THE HOUSE

Perhaps one of the greatest innovations in everyday life has been the use of electricity. We use it to cook, clean, watch television, and charge electronic devices without giving it much thought. But the way that electricity is brought into our homes has a fascinating story. It involves a feud between two of the most famous inventors of all-time: Thomas Edison (1847–1931) and Nikola Tesla (1856–1943).

In the 1880s, no pair of inventors captured the imagination of people quite like Edison and Tesla. Edison, who was mostly self-taught, was a slow and deliberate explorer of the world around him. He worked tirelessly, but had little knowledge of the mathematics and scientific formulas behind the work he was doing.

Tesla, a onetime pupil and employee of Edison, was a much flashier inventor with years of formal education. Instead of working by **trial and error**, Tesla applied his skills in engineering and mathematics to improve his inventions. Tesla often overshadowed Edison by beating him to new discoveries. But their biggest clash came over two rival forms of **transmitting** electrical power—direct current (DC) and alternating current (AC).

DID YOU KNOW?

The feud between the Edison and Tesla was actually referred to as the "War of Current." Both types of current are still being used today.

What is the difference between DC and AC? Direct current is **electrical current** that flows only in one direction. Batteries, **fuel cells**, and **solar cells** produce and use DC because they have positive and negative terminals. The current always flows in the same direction between those terminals.

Alternating current flows in both directions, and it changes direction periodically. While AC works better for traveling long distances through power lines, the higher **voltage** of its current makes it very dangerous. DC power usually has a lower voltage, making it great for items we use every day. Edison and Tesla publicly argued over which method was better.

In the end, Tesla's AC won out, thanks to its ability to transmit power long distances without losing a lot of energy.

However, Edison's DC wasn't completely defeated. It's used today in many devices in the home. Have you ever noticed the "power brick" on cables used to charge devices, such as cell phones? Those bricks convert AC power from the wall socket to DC power for devices. You can thank both men for the electrified homes we live in today!

A BRIGHT IDEA

Are you reading this book with the lights on? Edison generally gets the credit for inventing the light bulb, but he was just one of many people who worked on this technology. As early as 1802, a British inventor named Humphry Davy (1778–1829) created the electric arc lamp, which produced light between two carbon rods. It worked, but was very hard to manufacture.

WORDS TO KNOW

filament: a slender, threadlike fiber.

incandescent: a source of electric light that works by heating a filament.

lapse: to stop or end.

Working hard to improve the technology, Edison and his researchers discovered that a carbon **filament** made the best **incandescent** light bulb. But there was problem—the light bulbs didn't last very long and were expensive to replace. It was thanks to an inventor named Lewis Howard Latimer (1848–1928) that a more efficient means of making these filaments was patented.

The son of escaped slaves from the American South, Latimer was a gifted draftsman and engineer. While working for a competitor of Edison's company, he designed a way of protecting the delicate carbon filament by surrounding it with a cardboard envelope. This simple answer to a complex problem brought Latimer to the attention of Edison, who hired Latimer to work in his laboratory. Latimer later created a safety system for elevators and an early version of today's air conditioner.

An English chemist named Joseph Swan (1828–1914) invented a working lightbulb in 1850, but its technology was too expensive to market.

DID YOU KNOW?

The process of improving on the light bulb hasn't ended yet—today, innovators are developing even more efficient ways of producing light, including compact fluorescent bulbs (CFLs) and light-emitting diodes (LEDs).

CREATING CONVENIENCE

Imagine going for a car ride in the pouring rain. What's one of the first things the driver will do? Thanks to Mary Anderson (1866–1953), they'll turn on their windshield wipers.

Anderson came up with the idea of windshield wipers around the year 1900, when she was riding on a streetcar during a storm. She watched the driver lean out his window to clear off the windshield so he could see. Anderson went home and drew a design for

a blade that would wipe snow, sleet, and rain from the windshield. Her wipers would be operated by hand from inside the vehicle, allowing the driver to stay safely inside while it was moving.

She received a patent for her idea, but she was unable to get anyone to buy it. They claimed that it would distract drivers, and couldn't possibly remove the amount of water and ice she claimed. Unfortunately, the patent **lapsed** and she never earned money from an invention we now take for granted.

BAG IT UP

How do you carry your groceries home? Many people use flat-bottomed paper bags that are also great for covering your school books. These bags were invented by Margaret Knight (1838–1914), who began inventing things at a young age. When she was 12, she saw an accident at a textile mill. She realized that the machines kept working, even if something fell into them.

Knight designed a device to stop the machinery automatically if something was caught, greatly improving worker safety. By the time she was in her teens, her invention was being used in many textile mills across the United States to prevent accidental injuries.

When Knight went to work in a paper bag factory, she realized that all the bags were made flat and could not be opened up for easy packing. Determined to find a better way, Knight invented a flat-bottomed paper bag and a machine that could fold and glue these bags.

When a man attempted to steal her idea, claiming that a woman wasn't capable of designing such a complex machine, Knight took him to court and won. She received a patent for her bag-making machine in 1871.

AN ISSUE OF TISSUE

How much thought have you given to toilet paper? It's something that most people don't think much about, at least until they run out! But before the 1850s, most people used pages torn from magazines or newspapers to clean up after a trip to the bathroom.

Sometimes, people used even stranger things for toilet paper, such as corncobs, leaves, and even sand.

In 1857, Joseph Gayetty (1827–?) thought of a more comfortable way to clean up. The first toilet paper in the United States came in flat sheets and was sometimes medicated with **aloe**. Although it wasn't an overnight success, others improved upon the idea.

44

In 1871, Seth Wheeler added a few useful techniques, including wrapping the paper on a spool or roll and **perforating** the sheets so they tore off more easily. Later, innovators would produce toilet paper that was softer, scented, and white, creating the bathroom tissue we're used to today.

DIAPER DUTY

One of the most time-consuming and least-fun tasks for new parents is changing diapers. Before the invention of **disposable** diapers, having a baby meant constantly changing and washing cloth diapers. Fed up with the practice, a young mother in Connecticut named Marion Donovan (1917–1998) decided to make something more convenient.

Already someone with a flair for inventing useful things such as waterproof diaper covers, Donovan came up with her first disposable diaper around 1950. She created a diaper that was both **absorbent** and could be thrown away instead of washed. She used a special kind of paper that would not only absorb waste, but also keep wetness away from a baby's skin.

A patent gives the inventor the rights to the object they have patented. It means that no one else can make or sell it for 20 years.

DID YOU KNOW?

At first, she wasn't successful finding a company to manufacture her idea, but in 1961, the first disposable diapers made it into stores. Donovan went on to earn 20 patents for her ideas, but the disposable diaper remains the most popular.

Besides diapers, there are a lot of inventions around the house that save us time—but you might be surprised with how they came to be.

microwave: radiation with short wavelengths.

physicist: a scientist who studies matter, energy, and forces.

radar: a system for detecting aircraft, ships, and other objects, that uses pulses of electromagnetic waves.

WORDS TO KNOW

LABOR SAVERS

If you've ever been in a rush to eat, a microwave can be a big help. Before its invention, cooking required an oven or a stove, as well as time and patience. Today, almost everything can be heated more quickly using a **microwave** oven. And yet the invention of this time-saving kitchen appliance was actually an accident!

Percy Spencer (1894–1969) was working for a company called Raytheon in 1945. A **physicist**, he was an expert in **radar**, a new technology used to detect airplanes at great distances during World War II. One day, Spencer was standing in front of an active radar set when the candy bar in his pocket melted. Knowing that the heat of his pocket wasn't enough to ruin his snack, he suspected the radar system. He and his coworkers began experimenting to see if the radar waves would heat other foods.

One of the first things they tried was popcorn kernels, which popped and resulted in the world's first microwave popcorn!

He also placed an egg inside a kettle, making a hole in the side to allow the microwaves in. The egg exploded in the face of a coworker, who was looking into the kettle from the top. Despite this setback, Spencer realized that microwaves could raise the internal temperature of food much more quickly than standard cooking techniques.

He soon developed an enclosed metal box that would contain the microwaves more safely. Raytheon filed a patent for the first microwave oven in 1945, calling it the Radarange. It was 6 feet tall, weighed about 750 pounds, and cost $5,000 (about $65,000 today!). Does that sound like the microwave you use to heat up your leftovers? More than 20 years passed before microwave ovens became affordable and popular—around 1967.

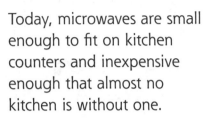

Today, microwaves are small enough to fit on kitchen counters and inexpensive enough that almost no kitchen is without one.

DID YOU KNOW?

CLEANING UP

After you eat your warmed-up leftovers, do you use a dishwasher? Washing dishes is one of those chores that can't be avoided. But thanks to an inventor named Josephine Cochrane (1839–1913), there's a machine that does it faster and more easily than washing by hand.

A man named Joel Houghton invented a dishwashing machine in 1850. It was made of wood and had a hand-cranked wheel that splashed water on the dishes, but it really didn't do a good job of getting them clean. Cochrane supposedly said in disgust, "If nobody else is going to invent a dishwashing machine, I'll do it myself." And she did. Cochrane was a homemaker, but after the death of her husband, she needed money. She hoped that her dishwasher invention would bring her some income.

In 1886, she improved on Houghton's idea and invented the world's first practical dishwashing machine. It had wire compartments to hold the dirty dishes, which were sprayed with hot, soapy water. This early dishwasher was mechanical and powered by a hand crank.

Cochrane **debuted** her dishwasher at the 1893 Chicago World's Fair, and at first, only hotels and restaurants were interested. It wasn't until the 1950s that dishwashers really became popular in homes. Cochrane started her own company, KitchenAid, which still produces dishwashers and other **appliances**.

While these appliances are definitely a big help, there are smaller innovations that might go unnoticed every day—but you might find it hard to live without them!

MAKING LIFE EASIER

Some innovators focused on how something was done, not just on new products. Lillian Gilbreth (1878–1972) was an expert in motion study and management. Along with her husband, Frank Gilbreth (1868–1924), she was interested in how to make everyday tasks around the house easier and more **efficient**.

Beginning in the 1920s, she invented a trash can that operated with a foot pedal, refrigerator door shelves for eggs and butter (refrigerator doors used to be flat), and a better electric can opener. Most importantly, she worked with hundreds of women to determine the most efficient and least tiring height for appliances, countertops, and tables.

Cheaper by the Dozen

Lillian Gilbreth managed a full-time career, housekeeping, and her 12 children. She and her husband, Frank, experimented with many ways to make household routines easier. Two of the Gilbreth children, Frank Jr. and Ernestine, wrote books about what it was like growing up in the Gilbreth household: *Cheaper by the Dozen* and *Belles on Their Toes*.

You can visit the National Museum of American History's online exhibit about the Gilbreths and their work here.

National Museum of American History Gilbreths 🔍

Some innovators found ways to improve people's lives in different ways. Sarah Breedlove (1867–1919), who was better known as Madam C.J. Walker, suffered from a scalp condition that resulted in the loss of much of her hair. In 1905, she invented a line of hair care products made especially for African-American women. She didn't just invent the products, but also traveled the country giving demonstrations to promote them.

She eventually established her own laboratory, which also developed cosmetics. She pioneered the training of beauticians who were taught to use her products and sell them at home parties in African-American communities.

Walker became one of the first American women to be a self-made millionaire. She donated large amounts of her money to organizations that helped African Americans.

What about innovations in how we eat? At the grocery store, you could get lost looking at all the different options. Have you ever wondered how some of your favorite snacks came to be?

Madam C.J. Walker's home parties were the first use of home sales parties, which are still used today for many products, including cosmetics, kitchen utensils, candles, and gift items. Why do you think this method of selling is popular?

DID YOU KNOW?

NEW WAYS TO SNACK

It's hard to imagine life without chocolate chip cookies, but they weren't actually invented until 1930. Their invention was by accident. Ruth Graves Wakefield (1903–1977)

and her husband operated the Toll House Inn in Massachusetts. Wakefield did all the cooking for the inn's guests. She was especially known for her wonderful desserts.

One day, she decided to make a batch of chocolate butter drop cookies, a favorite old-fashioned recipe, but she discovered that she was out of the baker's chocolate the recipe called for. She did have a bar of semi-sweet chocolate that the Nestlé food company had given her, so she decided to chop it up and add it to the recipe. She assumed the chocolate would melt and spread through the cookies.

Instead, the pieces held together and the chocolate chip cookie was born. The cookies were so popular that Wakefield published the recipe in several New England newspapers, calling them "chocolate crunch cookies." Sales of Nestlé chocolate grew dramatically. Nestlé made a deal with Wakefield that, in exchange for a lifetime's free supply of chocolate, it could print her recipe on its chocolate packages.

In 1939, Nestlé starting selling pre-chopped chocolate, today's chocolate chips. The recipe for Toll House Cookies, which still appears on Nestlé's chocolate chip packages, is Wakefield's original recipe. Today, 7 billion chocolate chip cookies are eaten around the world every year.

The man who invented potato chips had the appropriate name of George Crum (1824–1914). The year was 1853, and Crum was a chef in a restaurant in the resort town of Saratoga Springs, New York. One of the restaurant's specialties was fried potatoes. According to the story, a customer ordered the fried potatoes one night, but sent them back to Crum several times because, he complained, the potato slices were too thick.

Ice Cream Accident

There are several favorite foods that were invented by accident. The ice cream cone was invented in St. Louis, Missouri, in 1904, at the World's Fair, when ice cream seller Arnold Fornachou ran out of dishes for his ice cream. A neighboring vendor selling pastries, Ernest Hamwi, rolled up one of his round, waffle-like pastries, making it into a cone shape that would hold the ice cream. Fornachou's business flourished with this new invention, the ice cream cone.

Finally, Crum cut the potatoes into very thin slices, fried them in a vat of oil, and salted them heavily. He sent them back to the customer, thinking that they were now inedible and the customer would get what he deserved.

But the customer loved the thin, crunchy potato slices, and the Saratoga Chip was born. Historians aren't entirely sure that Crum was the first to invent the potato chip or that this story ever actually took place, but it has become the accepted story of the invention of potato chips.

While some inventors have found ways to take every-day objects and turn them into something new, it's likely that nobody beats George Washington Carver and the peanut.

Legends are often part of the story of invention. Does the exact truth matter when discussing invention history? Why or why not?

DID YOU KNOW?

CARVING OUT A PLACE IN HISTORY

George Washington Carver was born to slaves sometime between 1861 and 1864 in the Southern state of Missouri. Kidnapped at a young age with his mother and sister, Carver was eventually returned to his owners, but the rest of his family never made it home. With the abolishment of slavery in 1865, Carver's now former owners decided to raise and educate the orphan on their farm.

Later, after being rejected by colleges because of his race, Carver eventually received his bachelor's and master's degrees from Iowa State Agricultural College. He studied botany and made a name for himself as a scientist.

In the late-nineteenth and early-twentieth centuries, cotton was the main crop grown in the South. Used in many products, including clothing and packaging, it had been farmed by so many people for so long that the soil became **depleted** of the nutrients cotton needed to grow. Carver taught farmers how to grow crops other than cotton, rotating plants to keep soil from losing too many nutrients. His work helped many poor **sharecroppers** and former slaves earn a living as free men and women.

But Carver's most famous innovation was in the use of the humble peanut.

He developed hundreds of uses for peanut crops, from plastics, printer's ink, axle grease, and soap to shaving cream, skin lotion, and cooking oil. Carver didn't invent peanut butter, but he did develop a version of it! These innovative uses for a simple crop helped Southern farmers expand their farms and businesses. Carver improved the lives of countless farmers across the American South.

Carver's expertise in botany and **agriculture** earned him a prestigious post at the Tuskegee Institute, a university founded to educate African Americans when many universities and colleges would not. He became a trusted advisor to President Theodore Roosevelt thanks to his knowledge of plants and nutrition.

When you have a snack of cookies or peanuts, are you watching television? Some people think that the T.V. was the greatest invention of the twentieth century.

CHANNELING THE WORLD

What would life at home be like without a television? It's another invention that most people can't imagine living without, and yet a few generations ago, it did not exist. In the 1920s, many people were experimenting with methods of transmitting images that were similar to how sound was transmitted through radios.

A crude mechanical television, using a rotating disc with a spiral pattern of holes, was demonstrated by John Logie Baird in England and Charles Francis Jenkins in the United States.

The first patent for color television was granted to Guillermo González Camarena in 1940. The inventor and engineer developed a way to transmit color images that was used by NASA's Voyager space probes to send back the first up-close pictures of the outer planets! Camarena also built his own television camera from spare parts and junk—at the age of 17!

DID YOU KNOW?

But it was Philo T. Farnsworth (1906–1971), a 21-year-old inventor, who finally invented a working television. Farnsworth transmitted images using electron beams manipulated inside vacuum tubes. On September 7, 1927, he gave the first successful demonstration of television in San Francisco, California. Many innovators followed, improving Farnsworth's invention to make television what it is today.

Inventors and innovators have done a great deal to make everyday life easier, more entertaining, and tastier! What do you think our lives at home will be like in the future? What problems can you think of that need a solution?

ESSENTIAL QUESTION

Now it's time to consider and discuss the Essential Question: What do you think needs improving in your home? Can you think of a device you can invent to improve your own bedroom?

Home Kitchen Design

What invention could make your life in the kitchen easier? Take a look around your kitchen and spot the things that could be improved.

Think about what you do there every day, from getting a snack to helping make a meal to cleaning up. Now think of something that seems unnecessarily difficult or time-consuming.

* Do eggs fall out of the refrigerator door rack and break?

* Do cookies burn because there's no good timer?

* Is it hard to set the table because you can't get the dishes and silverware easily?

* Does it take too long to make your favorite drink or snack because you have to assemble the ingredients every time?

* Does your family throw out food because it spoils or you can't think of more ways to use it?

Choose a problem and then design a process or a device that can help solve that problem. Sketch a plan for your device, then construct it and try it out. Did it work to make a problem easier or solve it? Why or why not? How could it be improved?

Let's Make Safe Drinking Water

There's nothing more delicious than a tall glass of cold water when you're really thirsty. However, this is a luxury that many people in the world don't have. About 1.1 billion people around the world do not have access to water that's safe to drink. A girl named Deepika Kurup decided to do something about this. When she was in the eighth grade, she invented a water purification system that significantly reduces the bacteria in water, making it safe to drink. The best part is, her system runs on solar energy, so communities that don't have a steady supply of power can still produce healthy water. Kurup's next steps? "I want to start a nonprofit organization to deploy my innovation," she says.

Keep It Fresh

People have always tried different methods for keeping food fresh, including the use of salt. What methods work best for keeping food fresh and appealing?

Devise an experiment to test the preserving power of different substances. Some substances to test include lemon juice, vinegar, and salt water. See how well each of these substances preserves a piece of food, such as an apple slice.

Create an engineering design worksheet. What is the problem you are trying to solve? How will you keep track of your observations? What is a good way to test each substance? What will your control group be so you know how fast the food rots without any preservation?

Perform your experiment. How long do you need to leave your apple slices in the different substances? Which substance is best at preserving food?

TRY THIS: Try this experiment with different types of food. Do the preserving agents act differently on different foods? What about changing the location of the food in its preserving agent—does this affect the rate of decomposition?

ACTIVITY

The Nose Knows

Smell is a very important part of tasting foods and creating new recipes. What we smell—and taste—is because of the chemical properties of the foods we eat.

Some molecules are known as mirror molecules, or left-handed and right-handed versions of the same molecule. These molecules are made of the same atoms, but they are arranged in a different order. You can research more about mirror molecules at this website.

American History mirror molecules 🔎

Both orange peel and lemon peel contain a molecule called limonene. Using two bowls, grate a little orange peel into one bowl and a little lemon peel into another. Now smell each one. Do they smell the same? Can you discover why two fruit peels with the same molecule can smell different? What do the chemical structures of orange peel and lemon peel look like? What conclusion can you make from comparing them?

Now try the same experiment with crushed caraway seeds in one bowl, and crushed mint leaves in another. Both contain the molecule carvone. Do they smell the same? What do their chemical structures look like? How do they compare?

THINK MORE: Do some research and find diagrams of left-handed and right-handed limonene molecules. Consider that a left-handed carvone molecule looks like the diagram here. Can you draw a right-handed carvone molecule?

(S)

WORDS TO KNOW

properties: the unique characteristics of a substance.

Make a Solar Oven

In many parts of the world, where fuel for stoves or fires is difficult to find, people use the power of the sun to cook. You can make your own solar oven with cardboard, tin foil, black paper, and clear plastic wrap.

What form is your oven going to take? Where do the sun's rays need to go to warm your food? How can the black paper help? Remember, black paper absorbs heat, while aluminum foil reflects heat. How can you use these traits to cook food?

Once you have sketched out a design, try to build it. Test your solar oven on an apple slice, timing how long it takes the slice to roast. Does it work? How can you improve your design? What needs to change?

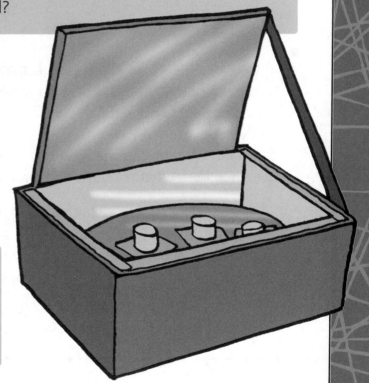

Build more of your designs until you create one that heats food quickly and thoroughly.

THINK MORE: How could you make this solar oven more powerful? Is it possible to cook things such as meat or bread in a solar oven? Why or why not?

Which One is More Efficient?

Is there a difference in efficiency between compact fluorescent light bulbs and incandescent light bulbs? Compare the heat created by each bulb to see which one makes heat more quickly and with less energy.

Caution: Be careful not to allow the paper to touch either light bulb. You don't want to start a fire.

Use a 60-watt incandescent bulb and a 15-watt compact fluorescent (CFL) bulb for your comparison. What do you know already about the energy these bulbs use? Position a desk lamp to shine up at a piece of paper. How can you arrange a sheet of paper so it is suspended without sagging above the lamp?

Once you have your experiment set up, place the incandescent bulb in the lamp. Using a dropper, place one drop of cooking oil on the paper and quickly mark with a pencil the diameter of the circle it creates. Turn on the lamp and wait five minutes, then mark the diameter again. How much has it changed?

Turn off the lamp and replace the incandescent bulb with the CFL. Using a fresh sheet of paper, repeat the experiment with the drop of oil. How much does the circle increase? Did the CFL bulb make the oil circle increase more than the incandescent bulb did? What does this tell you about the bulb's efficiency?

THINK MORE: Could you do this experiment with an LED light bulb? Why or why not?

Chapter 4

ENGINEERING NEW SOLUTIONS

Have you taken an elevator to the top floor of a building or watched crops being harvested? None of these things would be possible without engineers and inventors finding new ways to make things safer, easier, and more efficient. How would you like to be the person to design a new way of traveling? How would you like to figure out a way to make a dangerous task safer?

Farming is still a big part of America's economy, but in the early days of America's history, farming was one of the most common jobs people had. One crop in particular stood out from the rest—cotton.

ESSENTIAL QUESTION

If you were to design the transportation of the future, what would it look like and how would it be powered?

60

AN ENGINE FOR COTTON

Farmers grew a great deal of cotton in the years leading up to 1830, supplying much of the world with this crop. But getting cotton from the farm to a factory wasn't an easy task. Once it was harvested, seeds and other foreign materials had to be removed from the actual cotton **fibers**. This was a task that was slow and tiring when done by hand, and anything that is done by hand is often very expensive. It took the average worker an entire day to remove the seeds from a single pound of cotton.

Eli Whitney (1765–1825), an inventor and mechanic from Massachusetts, traveled to the South in 1792 and stayed on a plantation. While he was there, he heard about how time consuming it was to clean cotton and prepare it to be turned into clothing and other things.

It didn't take long for him to invent a machine to remove the seeds mechanically.

American farmers grew two types of cotton. Green seed, or short-staple, cotton did not need as much water to grow and was grown inland. However, it had more seeds and it was harder to pick those seeds out. Black seed, or long-staple, cotton could be grown in coastal areas and had fewer seeds.

DID YOU KNOW?

Whitney called it the "cotton gin" ("gin" was short for "engine"), and it worked by running the cotton through a wooden drum that had a series of hooks. The hooks caught the cotton fibers and dragged them through a **mesh** screen that was too small for the cotton seeds to pass through. Whitney's original hand-cranked gin could remove the seeds from 50 pounds of cotton in a day, a huge improvement on doing it by hand.

WORDS TO KNOW

Industrial Age: a period of time beginning in the late 1700s when people started using machines to make things in large factories.

nitroglycerine: a volatile yellow liquid used in explosives such as dynamite.

volatile: something likely to change quickly and unpredictably, usually for the worse.

blasting cap: a small explosive device that works with a fuse to ignite a much bigger explosive device, such as dynamite.

fuse: a tube or cord that is lit to set off an explosive.

Soon, larger gins were built, first powered by horses and later by steam power. Whitney patented the cotton gin in 1794, hoping to build gins all over the South. He envisioned farmers paying to have their cotton cleaned in a fraction of the time it took to be done by hand. However, many farmers simply stole the idea for the gin and built their own, so Whitney never made much money from his invention.

HANDLE WITH CARE

As machines such as the cotton gin grew more and more complex, people were coming up with new ways to harness the power of the **Industrial Age**. They also needed to come up with ways to protect people from that power.

Have you ever wondered how Mount Rushmore was made or how some highways seem to go straight through solid rock?

Who Really Invented the Cotton Gin?

No one is entirely sure if the idea for the cotton gin was all Eli Whitney's or if he had design help from Catharine Greene. Greene owned the plantation where Whitney came to stay and she was the one who explained the problem of cleaning cotton to him. Many historians feel that Greene actually designed the gin and Whitney simply helped her build it and then applied for the patent, since women were not allowed to file for patents at that time. Others believe that the gin was Whitney's idea and Greene simply provided a few suggestions for the design, as well as the financing. However it happened, Whitney got the credit and the patent.

You can see Whitney's original patent for the cotton gin here.

Eli Whitney patent 🔍

Sometimes, engineers use explosives to remove huge pieces of stone during construction—a process that was made much safer in the nineteenth century thanks to Alfred Nobel.

Alfred Nobel (1833–1896) was a Swedish chemist, engineer, and inventor. He was in the construction business, building many bridges and roads through difficult terrain. These projects often involved blasting rock away in order to build a foundation for a building, carve tunnels, or dig canals. At the time, one of the only explosives powerful enough to do this was a liquid called **nitroglycerine**. The problem with nitroglycerine is that it is extremely **volatile**—it's very easy to make it explode. Just the smallest bumping or jarring can set it off, making nitroglycerine very dangerous to work with.

Determined to find a safer way to blow things up, Nobel set to work on finding a new way to use nitroglycerine in construction. First, he invented the **blasting cap**, which used a strong shock to set off the explosions instead of heat from a lit **fuse**.

63

This gave engineers a much simpler and less-dangerous way of setting off explosions. But the biggest problem was the explosive itself.

With nitroglycerine so unsafe, Nobel tried many ways to make it less dangerous. He discovered that mixing it with silica, a quartz mineral that occurs naturally in sandstone and other rocks, created a thick paste. This paste could be formed into the shape of a **cylinder** and inserted into holes drilled in rock. This method was safer to handle than the liquid nitroglycerine and made it much easier to control the amount of explosive power used.

Later, Nobel invented dynamite sticks, which consisted of a cylinder, blasting cap, and fuse. Dynamite revolutionized construction and mining and made the process faster and safer. However, Nobel's invention was also used in an unintended way—in warfare.

SAFETY FIRST

Stephanie Kwolek (1923–2014) went to school to become a chemist. She started working for the DuPont company as a research chemist, something she intended to do only temporarily. But she liked it so much that she stayed. While at DuPont, she invented a new type of organic material, which turned out to have five times the strength of steel. The material is stiff but flexible, resists flames and **corrosion**, and doesn't wear out easily.

A Peaceful Payback

Concerned with how the world would remember him and his invention, Alfred Nobel devised a plan to reward people who tried to make the world a better place through science and leadership. Upon his death, Nobel's will declared that much of his fortune would be used to award prizes in physics, chemistry, literature, medicine, and peace. The first Nobel Prizes were awarded in 1901, and continue to this day.

Alfred Nobel's will 🔍

Kwolek named this new material Kevlar and she patented it in 1966.

Kevlar's most important use was as the main component in bulletproof vests. It is also used in underwater cables, brake linings, space vehicles, boats, parachutes, skis, suspension bridge cables, camping gear, and building materials.

New versions of Kevlar have been developed since Kwolek's invention, making it resistant to punctures and even stronger and more energy absorbing.

DID YOU KNOW?

Inventor Garrett Morgan (1877–1963) invented a very important device to protect humans from gases and other **toxic** fumes. Morgan was an **entrepreneur**, and by the time he was 18 he had already invented a chemical hair straightener and started both a sewing machine repair business and a newspaper.

In 1914, Morgan invented and then patented the Morgan Safety Hood and Smoke Protector—the first gas mask. It was a cotton hood with two hoses that hung down to the floor, allowing the person to breathe the cleaner air that settled underneath the damaging smoke and fumes. The hoses also had moistened sponge filters to screen out other harmful things.

Morgan would later modify the hood so that it had its own supply of air. When World War I broke out and chemical gas warfare became a common weapon, the Morgan Safety Hood was used as the basis for designing new gas masks to protect soldiers.

Morgan isn't remembered just for inventing the gas mask. He is also responsible for inventing a device that helps keep drivers safe on the road—the traffic signal. In 1923, Morgan witnessed an accident between a carriage and a pedestrian.

He realized that there needed to be a better way to alert drivers when to stop and go.

The idea for a traffic signal light was not new, but the existing signals indicated only "stop" and "go." Morgan's innovation was to include a third light, a yellow warning sign that would alert drivers to the impending change from one light to the other and give them time to react. Morgan's design was a T-shaped pole with three settings. When traffic was light at night, it could even be set to simply blink yellow. Can you imagine what driving would be like without the yellow "caution" light? What if there were no traffic lights at all?

GETTING FROM HERE TO THERE

If you were to design the transportation of the future, what would it look like and how would it be powered? In the days before the invention of the automobile, people relied on horses and boats for transportation. Early ships used sails to catch the wind, but when there was little or no wind, there was no reliable way to travel.

Safe and Sound

In 1916, Morgan's Safety Hood was used to rescue two men trapped 250 feet beneath Lake Erie in Cleveland, Ohio. The men had been working to drill a new water supply tunnel when they hit a pocket of natural gas. An explosion trapped the workers underground and exposed them to the dangerous gas fumes. When Morgan heard about the explosion, he and his brother put on their safety hoods and entered the tunnel. They were able to rescue two men and bring out four more bodies before the rescue effort was abandoned. The publicity from the rescue boosted sales of the hoods to firefighters all around the country.

Boats might also use **currents** and manpower to move them across bodies of water. In the late 1700s, a new type of power for boats was introduced—steam.

The first example of steam power was actually built in ancient Greece, but it was just a curious experiment at the time. In 1769, a Scottish inventor named James Watt (1736–1819) designed a powerful engine that could run on steam. Steam engines work by heating water, usually with wood or coal, to produce steam. As the pressure from the steam builds, it moves a cylinder that powers a **piston**—a little like bicycle pump.

locomotive: a vehicle that moves by itself and is used to pull railroad cars on a track.

propeller: a revolving shaft with blades, which moves a vehicle through air or water.

BCE: put after a date, BCE stands for Before Common Era and counts down to zero. CE stands for Common Era and counts up from zero. These nonreligious terms correspond to BC and AD. This book was printed in 2017 CE.

WORDS TO KNOW

This kind of engine was used for both railroad **locomotives**, where the piston made the wheels turn, and later in boats, where the piston turned a shaft that drove a **propeller**.

The first American steamboat was built by John Fitch (1743-1798) in 1787. He built four steamboats, but since they were expensive to build and run, they were not very successful. However, in 1807, another American inventor, Robert Fulton (1765-1815), built a steamboat called the *Clermont*.

On its first trip along the Hudson River in New York, the *Clermont* traveled 40 miles within eight hours, an amazing speed for the time.

It was the first successful use of steam to power a boat. Afterward, the *Clermont* and many other steam-powered ships made regular trips carrying people and cargo up and down the Hudson.

America's first steam-powered locomotive, the *Tom Thumb*, was built in 1830 by Peter Cooper (1791–1883). Just a few short years later, railroads began to crisscross the states.

Steam

Water

Combustion
Coal

Piston

Crankshaft

In 1869, the nearly 2,000-mile-long Transcontinental Railroad was completed, connecting railroads on both the East and West Coasts. Americans could now ride a train, pulled by a steam-powered locomotive, across the entire country. Steam-powered trains and boats were the fastest way to travel long distances in the nineteenth century, but the technology was also there to move people much shorter distances, too.

Heron Alexandrinus (10–70 **BCE**) invented a type of steam engine 2,000 years ago that consisted of a sphere on an axis. A fire beneath the sphere boiled water into steam. Two nozzles, located opposite each other, expelled the steam, which made the sphere turn around the axis.

DID YOU KNOW?

Streetcars ran on metal rails similar to railroads, but the rails were set into the city streets. The first streetcars were pulled by horses. In the city of San Francisco, which is known for its steep hills, it was very difficult for horses to pull loaded streetcars up the steep hills, even though the cars ran on metal tracks.

In 1871, San Franciscan inventor Andrew Smith Hallidie (1836–1900) invented a cable system, where the streetcars were attached to a metal cable loop that ran in a slot beneath the street. Powered by a steam engine in a powerhouse, the cables pulled the streetcars up the hills.

While steam power was eventually replaced by gasoline and electric motors, other inventors thought of new ways of moving people up through the floors of tall buildings instead of across the country.

hoist: to lift something using ropes and pulleys.

WORDS TO KNOW

hoist: to lift something using ropes and pulleys.

GOING UP?

As with many other kinds of transportation, the basic idea of an elevator to transport people up and down has been around for a long time. In 236 BCE, the Greek mathematician Archimedes designed a type of elevator that worked by using a rope wrapped around a drum, which was turned by hand. The Roman Colosseum used this kind of early elevator to hoist animals and men into arenas for horrific battles.

More modern elevators were first built in the mid-1800s. But because they were hauled up and down using regular ropes, which were easily frayed or broken, they weren't trusted for human passengers. In 1852, inventor Elisha Otis (1811–1861) came up with a device that made elevators safe enough for people to use. If the rope happened to break, springs would force open a set of levers called pawls that would hook into racks at the side of the elevator shaft. These kept the elevator from falling to the ground if the **hoisting** rope broke. This new idea fascinated engineers and architects, especially in cities.

Currently, the world's tallest building is the Burj Khalifa in Dubai, United Arab Emirates. It has 163 floors and stands 2,716.5 feet tall. Its elevators hold the world's record for the longest distance to travel, and climb at a rate of 33 feet per second.

DID YOU KNOW?

In 1857, Otis installed his first safety elevator in a five-story department store in New York City.

Its success made it possible for builders to start constructing taller buildings and eventually skyscrapers, since the upper floors could now be easily accessed. Without elevators, there would be no skyscrapers!

Another way inventors thought to carry people between floors was by using a "moving" staircase. But the first escalator wasn't really designed to be a people-mover. Instead, it was meant to be a new kind of amusement ride at the Coney Island amusement park in New York City. Inventor Jesse Reno (1861–1947) created it in 1895 and patented it as a steam-powered novelty ride.

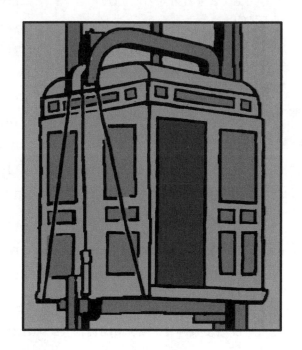

Innovator Charles Seeberger (1857–1931) redesigned the moving stairs in 1897 and gave it its name. He used the Latin word *scala*, which means "steps," and combined it with *elevator*, since that machine had already been invented.

Seeberger teamed up with the Otis Elevator Co. and produced the first working commercial escalator in 1899. Reno started his own company to produce them, although he eventually sold his patent to the Otis company in 1911.

Today, escalators are used in many public places to move people between floors of a building, and their advantage over elevators is that they can move many more people more quickly—you never have to wait to use the escalator!

In the twenty-first century, traveling to the top floor of a skyscraper is easy. You simply catch an elevator and up you go. But if you want to travel much higher or faster—to space, for example—you need something a little different.

friction: the resistance of one surface rubbing against or moving over another.

maglev: a transportation system where trains glide above a track using the power of magnets.

levitate: to rise and hover in the air.

repel: to push away.

WORDS TO KNOW

SPACE AGE TRAVEL

For many years, inventors and engineers have tried to find ways to make train travel faster and more economical. **Friction** between the wheels and rails of a conventional train makes it use more power in order to move. As early as the beginning of the twentieth century, inventors such as Robert Goddard (1882–1945) in America and Emile Bachelet (1863–1946) in France were exploring ways to create a frictionless train.

However, these two men were not successful at inventing a working frictionless train. The idea was not explored further until the Germans and Japanese started to do research in the 1970s.

One of the methods developed is the **maglev** train. A maglev train **levitates** above its guideway, or track, by the use of magnets. The magnets in the guideway **repel** large magnets on the underside of the train, forcing it to lift above the track. This eliminates the friction between the two surfaces.

Another system of magnets, powered by electricity, pushes and pulls the train along by alternating the electrical current between the forward and back magnets. Japan constructed its first test line in 1977, and maglev trains have been in commercial operation there since 1984.

"It is difficult to say what is impossible, for the dream of yesterday is the hope of today and the reality of tomorrow."
—Robert Goddard

Maglev in Action

Maglev trains operate only in three countries as of 2017—Japan, Korea, and China. Want to see a maglev train at work? Check out this video!

maglev video 🔍

While Goddard wasn't successful at creating a frictionless train, he is famous for another one of his inventions—the first rocket that used a liquid fuel made of gasoline and liquid oxygen. He'd been experimenting with rockets since his days as a student at Worcester Polytechnic Institute in Massachusetts, where he nearly set fire to the physics building by setting off a gunpowder rocket. Goddard continued to experiment with different types of fuel, and received two patents in 1914 for a liquid-propelled rocket and a two-stage rocket powered by a solid fuel.

sustainable: living in a way that has minimal long-term impact on the environment.

global warming: an increase in the earth's average temperatures, enough to cause climate change.

science fiction: a story set in the future about contact with other worlds and imaginary science and technology.

WORDS TO KNOW

When Goddard successfully fired a liquid-fueled rocket from his aunt's farm in Massachusetts in 1926, it was a moment just as significant as the Wright brothers flying the first airplane. He was one of the first scientists to propose that space travel to the moon could be possible using this type of rocket.

Goddard continued to work on developing rocket and missile technology throughout his life, but he died before the first manned flight of Yuri Gagarin in 1961. There is a crater on the moon named after Goddard, as well as the Goddard Space Flight Center in Maryland.

REUSABLE ROCKETS AND ELECTRIC CARS

Another inventor who has worked to improve how we get around is Elon Musk (1971–). Born in South Africa and now a Canadian-American citizen, Musk got his first computer at the age of 10. By the time he was 12, he had sold his first computer game, called Blastar.

After earning degrees in economics and physics, Musk went to Stanford University to start a doctorate degree in energy physics. He dropped out after just two days to start his own Internet company, Zip2, which provided content for websites. Later, he started x.com, an online financial services and payments website, which was sold and eventually became PayPal. In 2002, Musk started a third company, Space Exploration Technologies Corp., or SpaceX. He won a contract with NASA to deliver cargo and eventually astronauts to the International Space Station and beyond.

SpaceX aims to make spaceflight as cheap as possible by re-using its rockets. When most rockets are launched, they're left to crash back to Earth or burn up in the atmosphere. But SpaceX's rockets can fly themselves back to Earth, saving lots of money and making rides to space even cheaper. In March of 2017, SpaceX launched the first-ever re-used rocket—and landed it again!

But perhaps Musk's best-known company is Tesla Motors. Tesla is dedicated to making electric cars that many people can afford. It has released several different automobiles that can travel about 250 miles between charges and do not use gasoline engines. Tesla has also developed a self-driving car, as well as trucks and airplanes that run on electricity.

Musk says he has three overall goals for his companies. He wants to change the world and the people who live here by developing and producing **sustainable** energy, reducing **global warming**, and even preventing human extinction by setting up a colony on Mars.

At the moment, moving to Mars is still only **science fiction**. However, there are plenty of engineers here on Earth working to make our planet a better place, such as Egyptian teenager Azza Abdel Hamid Faiad (1996–).

A Different Liquid Fuel

To commemorate its famous student, the Worcester Polytechnic Institute holds a water rocket competition every year. Students from kindergarten through college are invited to compete by setting off their designs for water-fueled rockets. Since Goddard launched the world's first liquid-fueled rocket, the contest uses water for fuel, in part to avoid more Goddard-like explosions!

Robert Goddard archival footage 🔍

WORDS TO KNOW

biofuel: a fuel that comes directly from living matter, not from fossils.

catalyst: a substance that causes or speeds up a chemical reaction.

ethanol: alcohol made from plants that can be used as fuel.

Egypt produces about 1 million tons of waste plastic every year, which often ends up as trash on land and in the oceans. Faiad had an idea to turn waste, such as plastic, into a fuel.

The concept of breaking plastic down into **biofuel** feedstock, the raw material that biofuel is made from, was not a new idea. But Faiad used a new **catalyst** to break the waste plastic down. The catalyst, called calcium bentonite, breaks down plastic waste to produce gas products such as methane, propane, and ethane, which can then be converted into **ethanol**. Ethanol can be used much like gasoline.

Faiad estimates that this process could create about $78 million in biofuel, which would also help her home country's economy.

Faiad has applied for a patent for her process, and she won the European Fusion Development Agreement award at the 23rd European Union Contest for Young Scientists.

Science and technology have been the basis for many of the inventions of the twentieth and twenty-first centuries, including one that we can no longer even imagine living without—the computer. We'll learn more about that technology in the next chapter.

ESSENTIAL QUESTION

Now it's time to consider and discuss the Essential Question: If you were to design the transportation of the future, what would it look like and how would it be powered?

Build Your Own Maglev

IDEAS FOR SUPPLIES

AAA battery ✪ *8 neodymium magnets* ✪ *uncoated copper wire (25 feet, 18-gauge)*

Maglev trains use magnetic levitation to move vehicles without making contact with the ground. The word *maglev* is short for magnetic levitation. You can build your own version of a maglev train!

Caution: Since regular magnets are not strong enough, you need to use neodymium magnets. But neodymium magnets are very strong and may damage electronics, so handle them carefully!

Make your train by putting four magnets on each end of the AAA battery. The magnets need to be placed on the battery with the poles facing opposite directions. Otherwise, the train will not work.

Make the coils that will be your train's guideway. Cut a long length of copper wire and then create coils by wrapping it around an object slightly larger than your AAA battery train, such as a larger AA battery or a large marker or crayon. The coils need to be pretty close in size to your train, so don't wrap them around something too large.

Place your train inside the coiled wire guideway. What happens? Why does the train need to be made from a battery? Why can't it just use magnets alone? Why will the train only move in one direction? What could you do to make it travel in the opposite direction?

THINK MORE: How else can you reduce the friction between a train and its track? Can you think of other materials to use to create a vehicle that can levitate?

Exploring Steam Power

IDEAS FOR SUPPLIES

metal tube 🌀 *cork that fits tightly in the tube* 🌀 *two 18-inch pieces of stiff wire*

You can explore steam power by building a steam-powered rocket boat.

Caution: Ask an adult to supervise.

Put the cork in the end of the tube and make sure it's tight. Then carefully poke a hole through it with a nail or another sharp object.

Using the wire, wrap a piece around each end of the tube, about 1 inch from the end. Twist the wire tightly with pliers so that it won't slide.

Cut a boat shape out of material that floats easily. The boat should have a triangular, pointed front and a flat rear. Hammer a nail into each end to help stabilize the boat shape.

Use tea light candles, the kind that come in little metal cups. Place one candle on each end of your boat, using masking tape to stick them down. Then, place the metal tube so it is just above the candles, and wrap the wire around the boat to hold the tube in place.

Are you ready for some steam power? Carefully remove the cork from the metal tube, and fill the tube with very hot water. Replace the cork tightly and make sure that water can drip out of the hole in the cork. Why do you think this is necessary? What might happen if you don't put a hole in the cork?

Fill a sink or bathtub with water, then place your boat in it. Light the candles. What happens next? What process is happening? Why did you fill the tube with hot water? What would happen if you used cold water? What might happen if the hole in the cork is larger?

ACTIVITY

Spin It!

An inventor named Dean Kamen developed a scooter that uses a series of gyroscopes. These are spinning wheels that maintain their position in space even when they're tilted. His invention is called the Segway. Maybe you've seen people moving around while standing on a Segway? Gyroscopes help the Segway adapt and balance the rider. Try this experiment with a gyroscope to help you understand how they work. You can see people using the Segway at this website.

how Segway works 🔍

Start by finding some materials for your experiment. Most of them are inexpensive, or you might even be able to find them for free at a recycling center. You will need two plastic handles that can be screwed onto a threaded bolt on a bicycle wheel. The bicycle wheel can be found used or even borrowed off your own bicycle. You also need a stool or chair to sit on, with wheels, that moves easily. You might be able to think of something else to use if you can't find a chair. You'll also need a friend to help you.

Screw the handles, one on each side, onto the bicycle wheel. You might have to remove some of the outer nuts from the wheel to give you enough space to attach the handles. Then sit on your wheeled stool or chair and hold the bicycle wheel by the handles while your helper gets it to spin as fast as possible. Lift your feet off the floor and tilt the wheel in one direction. What happens? What happens if you tilt the wheel in the other direction? Can you hold the spinning wheel straight out in front of you? What happens then?

Think about how this experiment relates to the way a Segway works. How do gyroscopes make the Segway work the way it does?

THINK MORE: What other type of transportation could be improved or even invented using gyroscopic motion?

ACTIVITY

79

Aluminum Air Battery

IDEAS FOR SUPPLIES

aluminum foil ☙ salt ☙ activated charcoal (available at aquarium supply stores) ☙ 2 electrical leads with clips on the end (available from an electronics or hardware store) ☙ small battery-powered object, such as a holiday light or a small toy

It seems as though many of the things we use every day require a battery. It's possible to make batteries out of everyday objects, even if they might not be powerful enough to power your cell phone or your gaming controller.

Cut the foil into a 6-inch square. Dissolve some salt into a small cup of water. There should be enough salt so that it leaves a little on the bottom of the cup.

Fold a paper towel into fourths, get it damp with the salt solution, and place it on the aluminum foil. Put a heaping spoonful of the activated charcoal on top of the paper towel, and crush it gently with the back of the spoon until it is in very fine bits.

Pour a little bit of salt water on top of the charcoal until it is damp. Be careful not to let the charcoal touch the foil directly. There should be three separate layers, like a sandwich. This is your "battery"!

Take your battery-operated device and strip some insulation from the end of its wires. Then, take your electrical leads and clip one end to a terminal of the device, and the other to the aluminum foil. Clip one end of the second lead to the second device terminal, but press its other end firmly into the pile of charcoal. What happens next?

THINK MORE: Batteries convert chemical energy into electrical energy. How does the combination of salt water and charcoal create electrical energy? What chemical process is taking place? Can you use something other than salt water? Or something other than charcoal?

Who Was the Real Inventor?

Historians are divided as to who really invented the cotton gin. Was it Eli Whitney, with his mechanical abilities? Or was the gin really designed by Catharine Greene, the plantation owner?

With an adult's permission, research the invention of the cotton gin, online and at the library. Try to find primary sources about who designed this device. Some suggestions:

* The Eli Whitney Museum and Workshop
* National Archives
* Correspondence by one of Whitney's relatives

Eli Whitney Museum cotton gin 🔎

National Archives Eli Whitney's patent 🔎

correspondence of Eli Whitney relative 🔎

Write an argument for each role—Eli Whitney and Catharine Greene—about why they were the inventors of the gin. Include details about the engineering design process, where they got their inspiration, and more.

* Who do you think was the true inventor of the cotton gin?

* Is it easier today to know who thought of new inventions? What are some clues you can use to know?

* Why are sources important when studying a controversial topic? How can you tell if you are using a trusted online resource?

PS

THE FIRST COTTON-GIN.—Drawn by William L. Sheppard.—[See Page 313.]

African American slaves using the first cotton gin, 1790–1800

ACTIVITY

Problem Solving

Many innovators invented devices or processes because they saw a problem in their everyday lives and decided to do something to fix it. You can do the same thing.

Think about your everyday life: what you see, what you do, what happens around you, your regular chores and activities. Now think of something that is a problem. Maybe it's the fact that your household can't seem to sort recycling very well. Maybe you can't get drivers to slow down when they drive through your neighborhood.

Once you've decided on a problem, design a device, process, plan, or piece of equipment that can solve that problem. Write out your design and explain it if necessary. Then, build your device or find a way to make your plan happen. You might need to start with getting people to come together and help you.

Once you have a product or process that works the way you want it to, think of ways to sell it. How will you get the word out that this is something people might want to have? What kind of research can you do on your intended audience? If you are thinking of selling your invention, how much should you charge? How will you make it available for your customers?

THINK MORE: Does your invention lead to more innovation? Make your designs and plans available to other people and invite them to see what they can come up with. Remember, innovation is often based on the work of other people who came before you! Were you inspired by someone else's ideas?

ACTIVITY

Chapter 5

HANDS-ON TECHNOLOGY

GREETINGS FROM THE PAST!

Today, technology is everywhere and in nearly everything. We use it to stay in touch with friends and family, to get across town, and travel around—and above—the earth. However, not too long ago, people did not have computers and cell phones. Further back in history, there were no landline telephones or even printed books. The ways we communicate have changed, thanks to forward-thinking people who wondered, "What if . . . ."

How many books have you read in your life? Before the 1400s, books were rare and expensive objects. Written by hand, they had to be copied by hand.

? ESSENTIAL QUESTION

What do you think is the greatest technological invention ever? Why?

83

quill: the wing or tail feather of a bird, used as a writing pen.

vellum: fine paper made from the skin of a calf.

moveable type: metal letters that can be arranged in molds to form words.

pamphlet: an informative book or brochure.

literacy: the ability to read.

electromagnet: metal made into a magnet by passing electric current through it.

circuit: a path that lets electricity flow when closed in a loop.

translate: to turn something from one language to another.

WORDS TO KNOW

Because every book was copied by hand, it was easy for mistakes to creep in. It also took a long time to make a copy of a book using ink and **quill** pens on **vellum**. It was a difficult process, and meant that books were mostly available to the wealthy. Most people never owned a book in their entire lives!

MAKING AN IMPRESSION

A German blacksmith named Johannes Gutenberg (circa 1395–1468) changed that. He invented several devices that together created a system for printing books and other texts much more quickly and accurately.

He invented something called **moveable type**, a revolution for the printing industry. Metal letters were arranged in molds to form words, and used repeatedly to make pages. Inspired by farming presses that squeezed fruit to make wine, Gutenberg arranged the metal type in a press. Oil-based inks, also invented by Gutenberg, coated the type, and the press pushed these inked letters onto paper to create print. All of these inventions worked together to usher in the very beginning of the modern era.

Information in the form of books, pamphlets, and other texts could be produced easily and cheaply distributed to more people.

The last time a Bible printed by Gutenberg went up for auction, in 1978, the final price was $2.2 million. Experts estimate that a complete Gutenberg bible today would sell for $25 million to $35 million.

DID YOU KNOW?

Once the cost of printing words on paper came down, more and more people began learning to read and write. It was the beginning of a surge in **literacy** around the world.

Gutenberg created new ways of spreading information and ideas with the printed word, but in the nineteenth century, people wanted a faster way to communicate in a growing world—especially across oceans.

LONG BEFORE EMOJIS

Before there were cellphones and texting, Samuel Morse (1791–1872) invented a way to send messages long distances through wires. These messages could be anything from the latest news to personal notes—and even secret codes.

Americans Samuel Morse, Joseph Henry (1797-1878), and Alfred Vail (1807-1859) built the first telegraph in 1836. This system sent pulses of electric current along wires to an **electromagnet** at the other end. A buzzing or clicking sound occurred when the **circuit** was completed, signaling a connection. But there was a problem—they needed some sort of code to **translate** words into the electrical pulses that traveled along the wires.

transcribe: to put thoughts, speech, or data into writing.

fluent: able to express oneself easily in another language.

decipher: to figure out the meaning of something.

intercept: to prevent something from continuing to a destination.

WORDS TO KNOW

So Morse invented a code that used the pulses and the spaces of silence between them. He used long signals (dashes) and short signals (dots) to create letters and numbers.

The dots and dashes could be received and **transcribed** back into regular words at the end of the wire. The telegraph system required both the sender and the receiver

The first message sent by telegraph was written by Samuel Morse. It read, "What hath God wrought?"

DID YOU KNOW?

to be **fluent** in Morse code, and to many operators it became a second language. Even though other technologies have replaced Morse code, it is still used today, especially in navigation and when other, more modern forms of communication can't be used.

THE MOST IMPORTANT MESSAGES

In the nineteenth century, Morse code was vital for communications of every kind. But in times of war, and for secret communications between governments, officials, and spies, a code that everyone knew wasn't very useful. Secret codes, and the ability to **decipher** them, became important in many conflicts around the world.

One era in history when codes were matters of national security was during World War II. The Allied powers, which included the United States, Britain, France, USSR, and Australia, fought against the Axis powers—Germany, Italy, and Japan. Each side communicated in code, and governments dedicated lots of resources and entire departments to the task of deciphering the enemy's codes.

The most important code-breaking organization for the Allies was located at Bletchley Park in England. Here, nearly 10,000 people worked during the war to **intercept** and decode messages from the enemy. They also used codes to feed misinformation back to the enemy.

About 75 percent of the Bletchley Park codebreakers were women. Some were already in the military, but many were recruited from schools and colleges at a young age because they were good at math or solving crosswords and other puzzles. Women such as Mavis Lever (1921–2013), Joan Clarke (1917–1996), Margaret Rock (1903–1983), and Audrey Ruth Briggs (1920–2005) were instrumental in helping to break even the most difficult codes of the Axis powers.

A Different Kind of Click

In 1844, Morse sent his first telegram message in code from Washington, DC, to Baltimore, Maryland. By 1866, there were telegraph lines running under the Atlantic Ocean, connecting the United States to Europe. Until the invention of the telephone, the telegraph was the best way to send messages across long distances. The telegraph also laid the groundwork for many of the technological innovations that would follow. It was the beginning of the modern era of fast communication. Watch this video made in the 1950s about the impact the telegram had on history.

telegram history video 🔍

87

encrypt: to turn into code or a coded signal.

cipher: a hidden message.

torpedo: a cigar-shaped underwater missile.

WORDS TO KNOW

The codebreakers at Bletchley Park eventually cracked the German Enigma machine, a device that was used to **encrypt** Germany's messages. The Enigma was difficult to break because it had a **cipher** that was changed every day, making the machine capable of 159 million million million settings.

It was this nearly all-female team of codebreakers, working with master codebreakers Dilly Knox (1884–1943) and Alan Turing (1912–1954), who finally cracked the secret of the Enigma machine in 1941. Deciphering the code let the Allies learn about the German spy network in England and even feed incorrect information back to the

German military. Many of these women continued to work in codebreaking and other government roles after the war was over.

Transmitting codes and communications through radio and cable eventually led to even more ways of communicating across great distances, such as the cellphone.

A NEW WORLD OF COMMUNICATING

Many people consider printed books, telegraphs, and faxes as old technologies, especially in a world of cellphones and social media. But they have led to innovations that are an indispensable part of our lives today.

Wi-Fi for Videogames

Do you use Wi-Fi? Some of the technology used in Wi-Fi was invented by Hedy Lamarr (1914–2000) during World War II. Lamar invented an anti-jamming device that kept **torpedoes** on course. Today, her "spread-spectrum" idea helps Wi-Fi and Bluetooth networks reach the speeds we need to play games and stream movies. Lamarr also happened to be a famous Hollywood actress!

Morse could not have imagined that, one day, people could carry a device in their pockets that would let them see and hear someone on the other side of the world.

In 1973, the first call from a portable cellular phone was made by engineer Martin Cooper (1928–). Heavy and the size of a brick, that phone is a distant relative of the sleek machines many people carry around in their pockets.

Cellphones work on a network of transmitting towers. These towers transmit to and from cellphones, with the cellphone switching to the nearest tower in order to have the best connection. Cellphones have had an enormous impact around the world, especially in developing countries. Connecting remote villages to telephone lines is expensive, but constructing transmitting towers is easier and cheaper.

This has given people in isolated areas access to communication, news, and even the Internet. Many manage their businesses completely through their phone, transferring money and information to customers on the other end. Cellphones have become so advanced that they can handle most of the everyday tasks that computers do—sending email, reading documents, and editing pictures.

input: to put data into a computer.

programming: the act of creating computer programs.

WORDS TO KNOW

But before we had laptops and desktops, the word "computer" meant something very different from what we mean when we talk about the machines we use today.

EARLY COMPUTERS

In the early 1800s, a computer was what people called a person who spent their days adding and subtracting numbers. These people created tables of calculations for others to use. The word compute means "to calculate, to add up, to count." The first machine computers were called "automatic computers" to differentiate them from people.

Between 1833 and 1871, a British mathematician named Charles Babbage (1791–1871) worked on a design for a machine called the Difference Engine. This was the first device that was at all similar to a modern computer. It could perform addition and subtraction but not complex problems.

Building the Engine

In Charles Babbage's time, the existing technology was not far enough along to actually build his machines. Finally, in 2002, the Science Museum in London built the Difference Engine from Babbage's designs and specifications. It weighs 5 tons, is 11 feet long, and has 8,000 moving parts. It works through the movements of gears, rods, cams, and levers, and performs exactly as Babbage designed it to. The museum also has on display unfinished pieces of the Analytical Engine, as well as Babbage's actual brain!

You can see a second Analytical Engine replica at work here.

Babbage Difference Engine in motion 🔍

Babbage went on to design a more advanced machine called the Analytical Engine. It could also perform multiplication and division. The Analytical Engine had two components—the mill, which is like the central processing unit of a modern computer, and the store, which is like the memory. The design even had a reader for **inputting** information and a printer for storing it on paper. He had 500 pages of designs and instructions for the Analytical Engine, but Babbage never actually built a prototype.

Babbage had designed a mechanical computer, but computers don't work without the programs that tell them how to function. The pioneer in **programming** was someone Babbage happened to meet at a party, a woman named Ada Lovelace (1815–1852). She was a gifted mathematician who found herself interested in Babbage's ideas after translating an article about him from French into English.

In 1980, the U.S. Department of Defense named a new computer language "Ada," in honor of Lovelace and her work.

DID YOU KNOW?

Lovelace added her own notes and ideas about the machine, which were published in an English scientific journal. Among her ideas was creating codes for turning letters and numbers into symbols, a type of programming language. Another one of her ideas was that a looping, or repeating, set of instructions could be developed for the machine, similar to the way modern computer programs are written.

WORDS TO KNOW

commercial: sold to the consumer for a profit.

touchpad: a small touch-sensitive panel used for inputting and controlling a computer.

microprocessor: a small electronic chip that manages information and controls what a computer does.

Because of her ideas, Lovelace is considered to be the first computer programmer, even though her contributions were not discovered until the 1950s.

A NEW LANGUAGE

Once computers and programming became more common and their use more routine, innovators saw ways to make them easier to use, as well as more entertaining.

In the early 1960s, Douglas Engelbart (1925–2013), who was part of the Stanford Research Institute in California, was looking for a better way for humans to interact with computers. He had several ideas, including a joystick, a light pen, and the first version of a mouse. With funding from NASA, he and his colleague, William English (1929–), came up with a series of tests to find which device made moving a cursor on the screen easiest. The mouse outperformed the joystick and the light pen.

The first **commercial** mouse was shipped in 1984. Even with **touchpad** technology, the mouse is still popular today. You'll notice that the mouse has lost its tail and become cordless.

DID YOU KNOW?

The first prototype mouse was built in 1964. It was a wooden shell with two perpendicular discs that could be tilted or rocked to draw lines. Originally, the cord was in the front, although it was moved to the back to keep it from getting in the way. They called it a mouse because the cord looked like a tail coming out of the end. Today, the mouses on most computers are cordless.

A Book in a Tweet

Is it possible to write a book within the 140-character limit of a Tweet? Some authors have tried! They either write the novel through a series of Tweets or condense the plot of a book into just a line or two. Author Hari Kunzru (1969–) wrote an example:

> *I'm here w/disk. Where ru? Mall too crowded to see. I don't feel safe. What do you mean you didn't send any text? Those aren't your guys?*

Many critics feel that Twitter could create an entirely new category of fiction. What do you think?

Another innovator helped to make the Internet possible through his work with computer communication. Philip Emeagwali (1954–) was born in Nigeria, a country in Africa, and had to drop out of school at a young age when his father could not afford his school fees. However, he went on to earn degrees from several universities.

In the 1980s, as part of his studies, Emeagwali decided to see if he could use thousands of linked **microprocessors**, rather than using a few supercomputers, to solve advanced computing problems. He was able to not only link these processors, but also enable each processor to talk to six others at the same time. This created a huge web of communicating microprocessors.

It was an early version of what would eventually become the Internet. Emeagwali has won many prestigious prizes for his work, and is considered to be one of the "fathers" of the Internet.

contraption: a machine or device that may seem unnecessarily complicated or strange.

WORDS TO KNOW

From the first Difference Engine to today's supercomputers, computer technology has changed our lives in every way. But the use of computers really exploded with the Internet.

WHAT CAN YOU DO ONLINE?

Where do you shop? Do you go to a store or do you shop online? E-commerce, which is buying and selling things on the Internet, is a fairly new invention. The first e-commerce transaction took place in August 1994, when a man named Dan Kohn created an online shopping site called NetMarket. His first transaction was the sale of a music CD, accepting payment over the Internet.

Meanwhile, a young man named Jeff Bezos (1964–) was thinking about the possibilities of selling things online, too. As a kid, Bezos loved to figure out how things worked. He created

contraptions all around his house. He went to Princeton University and earned a degree in computer science and electrical engineering, and started working in finance.

He was intrigued by the idea of e-commerce. In 1994, Bezos quit his job, moved to Seattle, Washington, and started an online bookstore. At first, the company was located in his garage, but eventually he moved it into a spare bedroom. With just three computer stations, he created a test site and had friends try it.

On July 16, 1995, the company officially opened. Bezos named it Amazon.com, after the great river in South America.

Amazon was an immediate hit. In just one month, it was selling books all across America and in 45 other countries. In the first two months, sales reached $20,000 a week. Unlike some Internet startups, Amazon has kept growing successfully, expanding to include video on demand and the Kindle e-reader and selling much, much more than books. Amazon has even started making its own movies.

Bezos is currently experimenting with a new delivery service called Amazon Prime Air, which will use remote-controlled drones to make deliveries to customers. These delivery robots can carry items that weigh less than 5 pounds and fly within 10 miles of the company's distribution centers. How would you like to have a package delivered by drone?

A drone, technically known as an unmanned aerial vehicle, is basically a flying robot. They were first used by the military, but today they also do tasks such as search and rescue, traffic and weather monitoring, and firefighting.

DID YOU KNOW?

The Internet is for more than just shopping, of course. Innovators have found ways to make it even more useful by creating two companies that many people use every day—Google and Yahoo.

What's in a Name?

Larry Page and Sergey Brin considered calling their new search engine the Whatbox, but then settled on the mathematical term "googal," which is a number with 100 zeros. They changed the spelling a little bit and realized it was easy to type and would make a great name for their new way to search the Internet—Google.

In 1995, Larry Page (1973–) visited Stanford University in California as a prospective graduate student. His campus tour guide was Sergey Brin (1973–), who was a math whiz earning a PhD in computer science. The two men didn't get along and actually spent most of the day arguing. A year later, when they were both attending Stanford, they became friends who together would change the way the world uses the Internet.

Grace Hopper is usually given credit for coining the term "computer bug," after discovering that a moth had caused a short circuit in the Mark II computer she was working on at Harvard University.

DID YOU KNOW?

While working on a project, they realized there needed to be a better way to search the World Wide Web. They developed a ranking system to show the most valuable sites for any kind of search, from automobiles to zebras. In 1997, they launched both a company and a search engine named Google.

Since then, Google has gone on to create many different devices and applications that are used by people every day. If you use an Android device, that's a Google creation, too! Google also takes on new and different challenges under Google X. Also called the "moonshot factory," Google X is an experimental laboratory striving to find the next great innovation in technology.

Headed by Brin, Google X has created devices such as the smart glasses called Google Glass and artificial intelligence with Google Brain. The company is currently working on self-driving cars and giant balloons that bring the Internet to remote places!

But computers and the Internet aren't only for finding the best kitten videos or buying the latest gadgets. They're used for fun, too.

FUN AND GAMES

Which computer games do you like to play? Gamers can thank Steve Russell (1937–), who invented the first popular computer game, called *Spacewar!*, in 1962. Russell was a programmer who was inspired to create *Spacewar!* by the writings of the science fiction author E.E. "Doc" Smith (1890–1965).

Russell spent 200 hours programming the game, in which two opponents in spaceships fire photon torpedoes at each other. Besides being an entertaining game, it used an operating system that allowed multiple users to share a computer at the same time. The game was also eventually used as a diagnostic program for computer customers.

Fast forward to 1987, when computer programmer Amy R. Briggs (1962–) created an interactive computer game called *Plundered Hearts*. Briggs worked as a game tester for the Infocom company when she came up with the idea for *Plundered Hearts*, which rose partly out of her college degree in literature.

augmented reality (AR):
inserting real-world images into a
game environment or interacting
with real-world objects.

supercapacitor: an energy
storage device tiny enough to fit
inside a cell phone battery.

WORDS TO KNOW

Briggs wanted to write a game that was basically an interactive romance novel. The single-player game places the player in the role of a young woman in the seventeenth century who is on a ship that is attacked by pirates. It was the first game with a lead character who was always female. The game was packaged with tangible objects, including a velvet bag and pretend currency from a country featured in the game. Briggs invented the game because it was the kind of game she wanted to play.

In the summer of 2016, one of the most popular smartphone apps ever was launched—Pokémon Go. The game's creator, John Hanke (1967–), was another innovator who worked for Google and helped create Google Earth and Google Maps. Hanke created an **augmented reality (AR)** game called Ingress, and the head of the Pokémon company, Tsunekazu Ishihara (1957–), was a big fan. In 2014, Hanke released a funny video of a Pokémon character on top of a Google map. It gave him the idea for Pokémon Go, where players chase, locate, capture, and train Pokémon characters in the real world, using a special phone app for both Apple and Android phones. The game uses real locations and allows players to take pictures of their captured Pokémon in the real world.

Just a month after it became available, more than 100 million people all over the world had downloaded the Pokémon Go app.

DID YOU KNOW?

AR isn't just for games. The technology has allowed doctors to perform surgery using robot assistants and the latest cars have a "heads-up" display that projects information such as driving directions and speed in a driver's line of sight so they never have to take their eyes off the road. Can you think of any other uses for AR?

CHARGE IT!

Have you ever had the batteries run out on a flashlight, leaving you stuck in the dark? Or maybe you've forgotten to charge you phone before you leave for the day? All of these electronics in our lives require energy, and many use batteries. Scientists all over the world are constantly looking for new ways to store more energy in smaller and smaller spaces. And one of the latest breakthroughs has come from an unexpected place.

Eesha Khare (1995–) was a high school student in California in 2013, when, at the age of 18, she invented a **supercapacitor**. Most batteries today take hours to charge, but the supercapacitor Khare invented enables the battery to be charged in just 20 to 30 seconds and can last for 10,000 charging cycles.

Khare won a $50,000 prize at the Intel International Science and Engineering Fair to use toward her education at Harvard University. Afterwards, she told the press, "I will be setting the world on fire."

Innovators and inventors have given us technology that makes life easier and helps us use computers for many more purposes every day. And ideas can come from anyone at any time, even if they're still in school!

?

ESSENTIAL QUESTION

Now it's time to consider and discuss the Essential Question: What do you think is the greatest technological invention ever? Why?

Print it Like Gutenberg

Johannes Gutenberg found a way to make book printing faster and easier. While old wooden printing presses are hard to find now, you can experiment with printing on a small scale.

Using a Styrofoam plate or small piece of foam board, draw a picture or pattern or write on the surface. Press down hard enough so that the marks you make are carved into the Styrofoam. Remember, if you want your writing to print normally, what will you have to do with your letters?

Pour a small amount of ink onto a paper plate, then run a hand roller through the ink until it is evenly coated.

Using the roller, coat the surface of your drawing or lettering with a thin, even coat of ink.

Place a sheet of paper on the inked foam. Make sure that it won't move, and run a clean, small roller back and forth over it until every section has been pressed down.

Carefully peel the paper off the foam and set it aside to dry.

How is the drawing or lettering printed onto the paper? What did you notice about this method of printing? What kinds of printing do you think it is best suited for?

TRY THIS: Think of other ways to build your own printing press. Are there materials that will work better? Can you invent a method of printing large amounts of text?

ACTIVITY

Codebreaker

The people who worked at Bletchley Park during WWII were expert at breaking codes and creating new ones. Try your hand at one of the simper versions of coding, called the Keyword Cipher.

Look at this chart. The first column is the regular alphabet. A keyword, in this case DOG, is placed at the beginning of the alphabet in the second column of the chart. This shifts the remaining letters of the alphabet *not used in the keyword*. The letters that are not used in the keyword are placed in line in alphabetical order following the keyword.

Code the message: WAIT FOR ME

The code for this is: ZDKW HRU PF

If you want a friend to be able to decode your message, you must give them the keyword along with the message. How can you do this in a way that won't give away how to decode the message to just anyone? Is a cipher with a longer keyword more secure or less secure?

Now create your own keyword cipher and send a message to someone else.

THINK MORE: What other ways can you think of to encrypt a message into code? Think of other things that could take the place of letters in a text. What elements are needed to make sure that the code can't be broken easily?

Keyword

A	D
B	O
C	G
D	E
E	F
F	H
G	I
H	J
I	K
J	L
K	M
L	N
M	P
N	Q
O	R
P	S
Q	T
R	U
S	V
T	W
U	X
V	Y
W	Z
X	A
Y	B
Z	C

Remaining alphabet shifted three letters

ACTIVITY

101

Morse's Message

IDEAS FOR SUPPLIES

3-inch steel nail ⚙ clay or putty the size of your fist ⚙ insulated wire about 20 inches long, with the insulation stripped from each end ⚙ strip of index card 5 inches long and 1 inch wide ⚙ steel thumbtack ⚙ 3 or 4 large, heavy books or wooden blocks ⚙ D-cell battery

Samuel Morse's code, and the telegraph, were a huge innovation in communication for their time. You can try building your own version of the electromagnetic telegraph to send a secret coded message.

Looking at your materials and thinking about Morse's telegraph, can you brainstorm about how these materials can be used to create a version of a telegraph key?

Start by making an electromagnet using the nail and wire. How can you coil the wire around the nail and attach the ends to the D battery? You will want to leave at least 5 inches of wire on the top and bottom of the coil, and attach one end of the wire to the flat end of the battery with tape. You can use the putty or clay to make the nail, with its coiled wire, stand upright. It is your receiver as well as now being an electromagnet.

Push your thumbtack through the middle of the index card strip, about ¼ inch from the end. This will be your tapper.

How can you arrange the tapper and the receiver to work together to make a clicking sound? Where should the tapper be in relation to the receiver? Can you use the stack of books or blocks to hold the strip and the thumbtack above the receiver?

Touch the other end of the coiled wire to the positive end of the D battery. What happens? What happens when you take the wire away from the battery top?

ACTIVITY

A. –	N– .	0– – – – –	**PERIOD**
B– – . . .	O– – –	1. – – – –	. – . – . –
C– . – .	P. – – .	2. . – – –	
D– . .	Q– – . –	3. . . – –	**COMMA**
E.	R. – .	4. . . . –	– – . . – –
F. . – .	S. . .	5.	
G– – .	T–	6–	**QUESTION MARK**
H. . . .	U. . –	7– – . . .	. . – – . .
I. .	V. . . –	8– – – . .	
J. – – –	W. – –	9– – – – .	
K– . –	X– . . –		
L. – . .	Y– . – –		
M– –	Z– – . .		

The nail is acting as an electromagnet and attracts the thumbtack, which makes the clicking sound. If the thumbtack stays stuck to the nail even when the wire is removed, the gap between them is too small. If the thumbtack doesn't stick to the nail, the gap is too wide. What can you adjust to make the gap larger or smaller?

Study the Morse Code version of the alphabet shown above and compose a short message. Using the telegraph key you've just made, tap out the message and have someone else try to decode it. Then trade places so you are the receiver and they are the sender.

THINK MORE: Why was it necessary to have an electromagnet to receive the telegraphed messages from the tapper? What would happen if there was no electromagnet? Can you think of another way to transmit messages across a long distance using Morse Code?

ACTIVITY

Binary Numbers

Data in computers is stored and transmitted as a series of zeros and ones. This is called the binary system. How can we represent words and numbers using just these two symbols?

Cut out five cards from heavy paper. On one card, draw 16 dots. On the second card, draw 8 dots. The third card should have 4 dots, the fourth card should have 2 dots, and the last card should have 1 dot. Can you recognize the pattern?

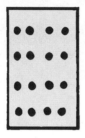 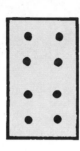   

Place the cards face up on a table with the 16-dot card on the farthest left and the 1-dot card on the farthest right. The cards should be in order in between. Flip the cards so exactly 5 dots show, but keep your cards in the same order. You have made the binary number for 5. The binary system uses zero and one to represent whether a card is face up or not. The number 0 shows that a card is hidden, and 1 means that you can see the dots.

* Find out how to get 3, 12, 19. Is there more than one way to get any number?

* What is the biggest number you can make? What is the smallest? Is there any number you can't make between the smallest and biggest numbers?

* Can you work out what 10101 is? What about 11111?

* What day of the month were you born? Write it in binary. Find out what your friends' birthdays are in binary.

THINK MORE: Try making the numbers 1, 2, 3, 4 in order. Can you work out a logical and reliable method of flipping the cards to increase any number by one?

Write Your Own Interactive Story

Interactive stories make great computer games because they change depending on the choices that the player makes. Try writing your own version of an interactive story with your friends.

Take turns opening the story and adding plot points, subplots, settings, characters, and twists. Where will your story begin? Who will be the main character? What is the first thing that is going to happen to that main character?

After the first person establishes the beginning, the second person can take over and make the storyline progress in a meaningful way. What happens next? Who else enters the story? Where does the story's tension come from? Does one character want something while the other character is standing in the way? This is called a conflict.

In 1962, computers were rare and it was expensive to use computer time for research. And yet, by the mid-1960s, almost every research computer in the country had *Spacewar!* installed on it.

DID YOU KNOW?

Keep moving through the story with each different contributor. The person who went first could be the person who goes last. How will the story end? What kind of resolution will you come up with? How are your characters going to get out of any jams they find themselves in? Are you going to leave opportunity for a sequel?

THINK MORE: Try this method of storytelling with different mediums. What would this look like as a computer game? As a play? A poem?

Chapter 6

INNOVATIVE ACCIDENTS

Not every invention or innovation has to be serious. Some are just for fun. And some inventions that started out as serious, turned out to be fun! Have you ever played with Silly Putty or Play-Doh? These two classic toys have something in common—they were both invented to be something else, and accidentally became popular toys.

During World War II, there was a shortage of real rubber because many of the countries that produced it were occupied by Japan, an enemy country of the United States. Without rubber, there was a shortage of tires and other products needed to fight the war.

? ESSENTIAL QUESTION

What is the connection between playing and inventing?

WORDS TO KNOW

synthetic: something made of artificial materials, using a chemical reaction.

An engineer named James Wright (1874–1961) was experimenting with ways to create a type of **synthetic** rubber. Wright worked at a General Electric lab in Connecticut. His job was to find something made from easily available materials that could be substituted for rubber. He decided to try adding boric acid to silicone oil. The result was a substance that seemed more stretchy and bouncy than rubber, but it was no better than the other rubber substitutes available at the time.

ACCIDENTAL TOYS

Wright did discover that this stretchy, bouncy substance had some interesting properties. When it was flattened onto a page from a comic book or newspaper, it could pick up the image as a perfect copy. Even though it was stretchy, it could break cleanly and even shatter if enough force was applied to it. It also was good for starting fires, because it burned fairly easily and slowly, and became white hot.

Wright called it "nutty putty" and shared samples of it with other scientists to see if anyone could come up with a good use for it. However, it seemed to only be good for entertaining people when he brought it to parties. Six years later, a consultant named Peter Hodgson (1912–1976) decided to market Wright's nutty putty as a toy. He changed the name to Silly Putty and packaged it in colorful plastic eggs.

Since then, Silly Putty has been one of the world's most popular toys.

People have found other practical uses for Silly Putty. It can pick up lint and dirt and be used to fix wobbly furniture legs. The *Apollo 8* astronauts even used it to hold their tools in place during the flight.

Play-Doh is another accidental discovery. In the early 1930s, wallpaper was a popular way for people to decorate their walls. Unfortunately, it was also the age of heating homes with coal, which left a layer of soot over everything, including walls. Back then, wallpaper was made of paper instead of the vinyl used today, and if the wallpaper got wet, it would come off the walls. A company in Cincinnati, Ohio, named Kutol came up with a formula for a wallpaper cleaner. Sales boomed until after WWII, when vinyl wallpaper was invented.

The Rubik's Cube puzzle was another accidental invention. Its creator, Erno Rubik (1944–), developed it to help his students learn about three-dimensional objects.

DID YOU KNOW?

How did a wallpaper cleaning agent become a toy? One of the company's owners, Joseph McVicker (1929–1992), had a sister-in-law who worked as a teacher. She gave the cleaner to her students to use as a modeling compound, and it worked so well she suggested to McVickers that the company market it as a toy. A few engineering changes later, a new toy hit the stores.

Today, about 100 million cans of Play-Doh are sold every year.

Slinky Jingle

"What walks down stairs, alone or in pairs, and makes a slinkity sound?
A spring, a spring, a marvelous thing! Everyone knows it's Slinky.
It's Slinky, it's Slinky. For fun it's a wonderful toy.
It's Slinky, it's Slinky. It's fun for a girl or a boy.
It's fun for a girl or boy!"

This song was written to advertise the slinky in 1962. In 1990, a newspaper called *USA Today* reported that of adults who were surveyed, 90 percent of them could sing the jingle! What makes it so catchy? Is it a tune you've heard before? You can watch the commercial here.

Slinky jingle commercial 🔍

In 1943, mechanical engineer Richard James (1914–1974) was trying to create springs that could be used to keep a ship's instruments and machinery from being damaged at sea. One day, he accidentally knocked some of his sample springs off a shelf. Instead of just falling, they gracefully "walked" to the floor. James and his wife, Betty, decided that his invention could be the next big toy. Betty named it the "Slinky."

Sales did not take off until Gimbel's department store in Philadelphia, Pennsylvania, allowed the Jameses to demonstrate the toy during the 1945 Christmas season. The first 400 Slinkys sold out in just minutes. More than 250 million Slinkys have been sold since then, and it is still a popular toy.

PLAYING WITH YOUR FOOD

Many toys have evolved into different versions from what they started as. Consider Mr. Potato Head. When this famous toy debuted, it would have been more at home in the kitchen than in a playroom.

George Lerner (1922–1995) was an inventor and designer who worried about kids not liking to eat vegetables. He thought that by creating a set of silly plastic faces that were shaped like pushpins and could be put on the vegetables, kids might be more interested in eating them. His original package, manufactured around 1950, had 20 different parts, along with a Styrofoam head to practice on.

It wasn't immediately popular, though, because many people had just lived through World War II. Parents did not want their kids wasting food by poking holes in it. Finally, Lerner agreed to let a cereal company use the pieces as giveaways inside cereal boxes.

Eventually, the toy company Hasbro bought Mr. Potato Head in 1952, and it was featured in the first-ever television commercial

for a toy. Soon, Mr. Potato Head was selling so well that Mrs. Potato Head appeared in 1953, followed by their children, Yam and Spud.

In 1964, the Potato family received plastic bodies and no longer needed real vegetables. Mr. Potato Head even appeared in Disney/Pixar's *Toy Story* movies. Today, Mr. Potato Head often appears as special edition characters, such as "Idaho Jones" (Indiana Jones), "Darth Tater" (Darth Vader), and "Artoo Potatoo" (R2D2).

BRICK BY BRICK

In 1932, in Denmark, Ole Kirk Christiansen (1891–1958) was making wooden toys in his workshop. He named his toy company Lego, from the Danish words *leg godt*, meaning "play well."

In 1947, Christiansen decided to branch out a bit. He bought a machine that could make things with plastic **injection molding**. He invented a set of **interlocking** building blocks, made of plastic, that he called Automatic Binding Bricks. The stud-and-tube coupling system was invented a few years later, in 1958.

Under the Lego factory in Billund, Denmark, there is a vault that contains one of every Lego set ever made, all new and unopened.

DID YOU KNOW?

The first Lego bricks were sold loose, but eventually the company created sets for making many different types of models. They added large Duplo bricks in 1969 and more technical sets with the Technic line in 1977. Lego also invented the Mindstorms system, which allows kids to build and program their own robots. Today, Lego makes sets from popular movies and characters, as well as their standard general building sets. They are still one of the world's most popular toys.

Lego Stats

Approximately 19 billion Lego elements are produced every year. Since 1958, more than 400 billion Lego bricks have been produced. That means there are about 62 Lego bricks for every person on Earth. In the United States, there are about 130 new Lego sets introduced every year. Around the world, about seven Lego sets are sold every second. The best-selling Lego set ever is the Lego Mindstorms Robotics Invention System. More than 1 million sets have been sold since it was launched.

HAVING A BLAST

Have you used a water gun to keep cool in the summer? There is one popular toy that was actually invented by a NASA engineer. As a member of the U.S. Air Force, Lonnie Johnson (1949–) helped develop the **stealth** bomber. In his work with NASA, he was a systems engineer for the *Galileo* mission to Jupiter and the *Cassini* mission to Saturn. One of his personal projects was inventing a **heat pump** using water instead of chemicals.

One day, he was experimenting with the prototype for this device in his bathroom. He pulled the lever and aimed the nozzle at his bathtub, and a powerful stream of water blasted right into it. It was so fun that Johnson developed it into a super squirt gun. In 1991, the Super Soaker topped $200 million in sales. That's a lot of soaked people!

As long as there have been humans, there have been inventors and innovators who have looked at the world around them and thought up ways to make life easier, faster, or more fun. Technology has increased the pace of inventions, and it seems as if there is something new every day. But none of the amazing things that come our way would be possible without the brains and imaginations of the people who dream up an idea and make it happen.

ESSENTIAL QUESTION

Now it's time to consider and discuss the Essential Question: What is the connection between playing and inventing?

Attractive Slime

IDEAS FOR SUPPLIES
bottle of white glue ☾ borax ☾ iron filings

You might have made your own homemade version of slime, made with borax and regular glue. White glue is basically a polymer, which is a long chain of identical, repeating molecules. The chemical in borax makes those molecules stick together and behave more like a solid than a liquid. But what happens if you add iron filings to a recipe for slime? Will it still act like a solid? How might this affect the slime's viscosity? Viscosity is how easily it flows. What will happen if you have a strong magnet near this slime?

Empty an entire bottle of white school glue into a bowl. Fill the empty bottle nearly full with water, put the cap back on, and shake it, to get every last bit of glue. Pour the water/glue solution into the bowl. Then add several tablespoons of iron filings to the bowl.

Measure ½ cup of warm water into a plastic cup. Add 1 teaspoon of borax powder, and stir it until it is completely dissolved. Then add this solution to the bowl. Mix the contents of the bowl with your hands until it looks like a familiar blob of putty or slime.

Find a very strong magnet, such as a neodymium magnet. What happens when you hold the magnet above the surface of your slime? How does the slime act? How does it change, depending on how close or how far the magnet is from the slime? Do the iron filings come out of the slime and attach to the magnet? Why or why not?

THINK MORE: Make a batch of regular slime, without the iron filings. Compare how it behaves when you pull or stretch it or put a magnet near it, compared to how the magnetic slime behaves. What is the same? What's different?

ACTIVITY

Slinky Science

Did you know that you can use a Slinky toy to learn about physics? This activity explores how the angle of a ramp affects how well a Slinky can walk down that ramp.

Slinkys are known for their ability to "walk" down a staircase or a slope. But do they walk better down some slopes than others, depending on the angle of that slope?

Design an experiment to test how quickly a metal Slinky can walk down a slope. You will need to be able to measure the angle of the slope and record the time it takes the Slinky to travel from top to bottom. What material will work best for the slope? What material will not work well?

Two classic toys, the Slinky Dog and Mr. Potato Head, were featured in the Disney/Pixar *Toy Story* movies. As a result, they became popular once again.

DID YOU KNOW?

Set up your experiment so that the slope can be easily adjusted and measured. How can you be sure to do the experiment the same way every time, only changing the slope? How will you record your findings?

Decide how many slope positions you want to test the Slinky on. Create a model for recording your findings. How will you time the Slinky's travel during the experiment? What did you discover as a result of your experiments concerning the movement of a Slinky and the angle of the slope?

THINK MORE: What happens if you do this experiment with a different material for the slope? Or when you use a plastic Slinky instead of a metal one? Can you design an experiment to test how well different Slinkys travel down a staircase?

ACTIVITY

abolish: to end something.

absorbent: having the ability to soak up liquid.

acceleration: the process of increasing the speed of an object's movement.

agriculture: growing plants and raising animals for food and other products.

air resistance: the force of air pushing against an object.

almanac: books of information about the natural world published every year.

aloe: the gel of an aloe vera plant, which is soothing to the skin.

anatomy: the branch of science having to do with the body structure of living beings.

anesthesiologist: a doctor who specializes in using medicine to stop pain or make someone unconscious.

antibiotic: a medicine that destroys microorganisms that cause illness or infection.

antiseptic: a substance that prevents the growth of disease-causing microorganisms.

appliance: a piece of equipment, such as a stove or refrigerator, designed to perform a certain task.

astronomy: the scientific study of the stars and planets.

atomic: having to do with atoms, the tiny particles of matter that make up everything.

augmented reality (AR): inserting real-world images into a game environment or interacting with real-world objects.

bacteria: microorganisms found in soil, water, plants, and animals that are sometimes harmful.

bacterium: a single bacteria.

BCE: put after a date, BCE stands for Before Common Era and counts down to zero. CE stands for Common Era and counts up from zero. These nonreligious terms correspond to BC and AD. This book was printed in 2017 CE.

bioengineering: the use of engineering principles applied to biological function to build devices, tools, or machines for a human need.

biofuel: a fuel that comes directly from living matter, not from fossils.

biomechanical engineering: the application of engineering principles and new materials to biology, especially to surgery and prosthetics.

blasting cap: a small explosive device that works with a fuse to ignite a much bigger explosive device, such as dynamite.

botany: the study of plants.

breeding: the development of new types of plants and animals with improved characteristics.

catalyst: a substance that causes or speeds up a chemical reaction.

celestial: positioned in or relating to the sky.

cell: the most basic part of a living thing.

chemotherapy: a treatment for cancer that uses chemicals.

cipher: a hidden message.

circuit: a path that lets electricity flow when closed in a loop.

climate: the average weather patterns in an area during a long period of time.

comet: a celestial object made of ice and dust.

commercial: sold to the consumer for a profit.

component: a part or piece of a larger whole, especially of a machine or a vehicle.

contagious: easy to catch.

contraption: a machine or device that may seem unnecessarily complicated or strange.

contribution: a part played by a person or thing in bringing about a result.

corrosion: the wearing away of metal by a chemical reaction. Rust is a type of corrosion.

crops: plants grown for food and other uses.

current: the direction in which water flows in a lake, stream, or ocean.

cylinder: a hollow tube shape.

debut: to introduce.

decipher: to figure out the meaning of something.

deplete: to use up, drain, or empty.

devastating: highly destructive or damaging.

diabetic: a person with diabetes, a disease that affects how the body uses blood sugar.

diagnose: to find and identify a problem.

disfigure: to spoil the looks of something.

disinfect: to clean something in order to destroy bacteria.

disposable: made to be thrown away after using once.

diversity: when many different people or things exist within a group or place.

drought: a long period of time when it doesn't rain as much as usual.

efficient: wasting as little time or effort as possible when completing a task.

electric current: the flow of an electrical charge.

electromagnetic: one of the fundamental forces of the universe that is responsible for magnetic attraction and electrical charges.

electromagnet: metal made into a magnet by passing electric current through it.

element: a substance whose atoms are all the same. Examples include gold, oxygen, nitrogen, and carbon.

encrypt: to turn into code or a coded signal.

engineer: a person who uses science and math to design and build things.

entrepreneur: a person who takes a risk to start a business.

environment: the natural world, especially as it is affected by human activity.

ethanol: alcohol made from plants that can be used as fuel.

evidence: the available facts or information supporting or denying a theory.

excommunicate: to officially exclude someone from participating in the sacraments and religious services of the Christian Church.

extinct: when a group of plants or animals dies out and there are no more left in the world.

fibers: long, slender threads of material such as wool or cotton that can be spun into yarn.

filament: a slender, threadlike fiber.

fluent: able to express oneself easily in another language.

fossil: the remains or traces of ancient plants or animals left in rock.

friction: the resistance of one surface rubbing against or moving over another.

fuel cell: something that produces a steady stream of electricity.

fuse: a tube or cord that is lit to set off an explosive.

geocentric: a model of the universe, now disproved, that the earth is the center of the solar system.

geology: the study of the earth and its rocks. A scientist who studies geology is a geologist.

germs: microorganisms that causes diseases.

global warming: an increase in the earth's average temperatures, enough to cause climate change.

gravity: a force that pulls all objects toward the earth.

habitat: the natural area where a plant or an animal lives.

heat pump: a device that transfers liquid from a colder area to a hotter area.

heliocentric: a model of the universe in which the planets orbit the sun and the moon orbits the earth.

hoist: to lift something using ropes and pulleys.

immune: the ability of a person to resist a disease or illness.

incandescent: a source of electric light that works by heating a filament.

incision: an opening made in the skin.

indigo: a tropical plant from the pea family that makes a dark-blue dye.

Industrial Age: a period of time beginning in the late 1700s when people started using machines to make things in large factories.

industry: a branch of business or employment.

infection: when microorganisms invade and make you sick.

injection molding: making objects of rubber or plastic by injecting heated material into a mold.

innovator: a person who introduces new methods, ideas, or products.

inoculation: a shot or medicine given to people to protect them from a certain disease or illness.

input: to put data into a computer.

insulin: a hormone in the body that regulates sugar in the blood.

intercept: to prevent something from continuing to a destination.

interlocking: things that connect, attach, or lock together.

interracial: existing between or involving different races of people.

irrigation: a system of transporting water through canals or tunnels to water crops.

iteration: the repetition of a process in order to make a product better and better.

Jurassic: a period of time that took place from 190 to 140 million years ago.

lapse: to stop or end.

levitate: to rise and hover in the air.

literacy: the ability to read.

locomotive: a vehicle that moves by itself and is used to pull railroad cars on a track.

maglev: a transportation system where trains glide above a track using the power of magnets.

marine: having to do with the ocean.

mass: the amount of material that an object contains.

mesh: material made of a network of wire or thread.

microorganism: a living thing that is so small it can be seen only with a microscope. Also called a microbe.

microprocessor: a small electronic chip that manages information and controls what a computer does.

microwave: radiation with short wavelengths.

minority: a group of people, such as African Americans, that is smaller than or different from the larger group. Minorities are often subject to discrimination.

mold: a furry growth.

molecular: having to do with molecules, the groups of atoms bound together to form everything.

moveable type: metal letters that can be arranged in molds to form words.

nanobot: a very, very tiny, self-propelled machine.

nanoparticle: a microscopic particle of matter.

naturalist: an expert in nature and natural history.

navigate: to plan and follow a route.

nitroglycerine: a volatile yellow liquid used in explosives such as dynamite.

nutrient: a substance an organism needs to live and grow.

observatory: a building with a telescope or other machines designed to observe objects in space.

organic: something that is or was living.

organism: a living thing.

paleontologist: a scientist who studies fossils.

pamphlet: an informative book or brochure.

patent: a right given to only one inventor to manufacture, use, or sell an invention for a certain number of years.

perforate: to make tiny holes in.

permineralization: the process of mineral deposits hardening within the tiny spaces of a dead organism.

pesticide: a chemical used to kill pests on crops.

petri dish: a circular, flat, transparent dish for growing microorganisms.

physicist: a scientist who studies matter, energy, and forces.

physics: the study of physical forces, including matter, energy, and motion, and how these forces interact with each other.

piston: a short, solid piece of metal that moves up and down inside a cylinder to create motion.

prediction: what you think will happen.

prehistoric: having to do with ancient times, before written human records.

prejudice: an unfair feeling of dislike for a person or group, usually based on gender, race, or religion.

product: an item, such as a book or clothing, that is made and sold to people.

programming: the act of creating computer programs.

propeller: a revolving shaft with blades, which moves a vehicle through air or water.

properties: the unique characteristics of a substance.

prototype: a model of something that allows engineers to test their idea.

pus: a thick, yellowish or greenish liquid produced by an infection.

quill: the wing or tail feather of a bird, used as a writing pen.

racism: negative opinions or treatment of people based on race.

radar: a system for detecting aircraft, ships, and other objects, that uses pulses of electromagnetic waves.

radiation: energy that comes from a source and travels through something, such as the radiation from an X-ray that travels through a person.

radioactive: describes a chemical substance made of a type of atom that changes because its positively charged particles escape from its center over time.

radioactivity: the emission of a stream of particles or electromagnetic rays.

reconstitute: to restore something dried to its original state by adding water.

repel: to push away.

rigorously: in an extremely thorough and careful way.

science fiction: a story set in the future about contact with other worlds and imaginary science and technology.

scientific method: the way scientists ask questions and do experiments to try to prove their ideas.

segregate: to keep apart.

sharecropper: a farmer who works on someone else's land and receives a small share of a crop's value after paying for tools, seeds, housing, and food.

solar: having to do with or produced by the sun.

solar cell: a device that converts the energy of the sun into electrical energy.

solar eclipse: when the moon passes between the sun and the earth, blocking the sun's light.

spear: a weapon with a long shaft and pointed tip, used for thrusting or throwing.

sphere: a round object, such as a ball.

spontaneous generation: an idea, known now to be not true, that life comes from something non-living.

stealth: technology that makes something hard to locate with radar or sonar.

supercapacitor: an energy storage device tiny enough to fit inside a cell phone battery.

sustainable: living in a way that has minimal long-term impact on the environment.

synthetic: something made of artificial materials, using a chemical reaction.

technology: tools, methods, and systems used to solve a problem or do work.

textiles: having to do with cloth and weaving.

theory: an unproven idea used to explain something.

tinkerer: a person who attempts to repair or improve something in a casual way, often to no useful effect.

torpedo: a cigar-shaped underwater missile.

touchpad: a small touch-sensitive panel used for inputting and controlling a computer.

toxic: something that is poisonous or harmful.

transcribe: to put thoughts, speech, or data into writing.

transfusion: the process of transferring blood into a human's circulatory system.

transit: passing through or across.

translate: to turn something from one language to another.

transmit: to broadcast or send out an electrical signal for television or radio.

trial and error: trying first one thing, then another and another, until something works.

vaccination: another word for inoculation.

vaccine: medicine designed to keep a person from getting a particular disease, usually given by needle.

vanquish: to thoroughly defeat.

vellum: fine paper made from the skin of a calf.

virus: a small infectious microbe.

volatile: something likely to change quickly and unpredictably, usually for the worse.

voltage: the force that moves electricity along a wire.

voracious: wanting or devouring great quantities of something.

zoology: the study of animals.

Metric Conversions

Use this chart to find the metric equivalents to the English measurements in this book. If you need to know a half measurement, divide by two. If you need to know twice the measurement, multiply by two. How do you find a quarter measurement? How do you find three times the measurement?

English	Metric
1 inch	2.5 centimeters
1 foot	30.5 centimeters
1 yard	0.9 meter
1 mile	1.6 kilometers
1 pound	0.5 kilogram
1 teaspoon	5 milliliters
1 tablespoon	15 milliliters
1 cup	237 milliliters

RESOURCES

BOOKS

100 Inventions That Made History. New York, NY: DK Publishing, 2014.

Casey, Susan. *Kids Inventing! A Handbook for Young Inventors*. San Francisco, CA: Jossey-Bass, 2005.

Currie, Stephen. *African American Inventors*. Farmington Hills, MI: Lucent Books, 2010.

Ideas That Changed the World. New York, NY: DK Publishing, 2013.

Spengler, Kremena T. *An Illustrated Timeline of Inventions and Inventors*. Minneapolis, MN: Picture Window Books, 2011.

Thimmesh, Catherine. *Girls Think of Everything: Stories of Ingenious Inventions by Women*. New York, NY: Houghton Mifflin Harcourt, 2002.

TIME For Kids Book of WHAT: Everything Inventions. New York, NY: Time-Life Books, 2015.

Wulffson, Don. *Toys!: Amazing Stories Behind Some Great Inventions*. New York, NY: Square Fish, 2014.

MEDIA

The History Channel: Inventions
history.com/topics/inventions

Biography.com: Famous Inventors
biography.com/people/groups/famous-inventors

Microsoft: What Are You Going to Make?
youtube.com/watch?v=Y8DBwchocvs

WEBSITES

National Inventors Hall of Fame: *invent.org*

MIT Inventor Archive: *lemelson.mit.edu/search-inventors*

The Black Inventor Online Museum: *blackinventor.com*

Famous Women Inventors: *women-inventors.com*

Smithsonian Institution - Women Inventors: *invention.si.edu/tags/women-inventors*

Popular Science Inventions: *popsci.com/tags/inventions*

Smithsonian Institution - Invention Stories: *invention.si.edu/explore/invention-stories*

Ducksters Biographies for Kids - Scientists and Inventors: *ducksters.com/biography/scientists/scientists_and_inventors.php*

Kids.gov - Scientists and Inventors: *kids.usa.gov/science/scientists/index.shtml*

Enchanted Learning Inventions and Inventors: *enchantedlearning.com/inventors*

National Geographic Kids - Black Inventors and Pioneers of Science: *kids.nationalgeographic.com/explore/science/black-inventors-and-pioneers-of-science/#black-scientist-jemison.jpg*

ESSENTIAL QUESTIONS

Introduction: What is the difference between inventors and innovators?

Chapter 1: How do recent medical discoveries build upon work done in the past?

Chapter 2: How does studying the natural world spark ideas for improvements in technology?

Chapter 3: What do you think needs improving in your home? Can you think of a device you can invent to improve your own bedroom?

Chapter 4: If you were to design the transportation of the future, what would it look like and how would it be powered?

Chapter 5: What do you think is the greatest technological invention ever? Why?

Chapter 6: What is the connection between playing and inventing?

QR CODE GLOSSARY

Page 17: anl.gov/articles/scientists-see-nanoparticles-form-larger-structures-real-time

Page 22: youtube.com/watch?v=oYEgdZ3iEKA

Page 25: transcription.si.edu/project/8045

Page 35: joshworth.com/dev/pixelspace/pixelspace_solarsystem.html

Page 37: zooniverse.org

Page 49: americanhistory.si.edu/ontime/saving/kitchen.html

Page 57: americanhistory.si.edu/molecule

Page 63: archives.gov/education/lessons/cotton-gin-patent

Page 65: nobelprize.org/alfred_nobel/will

Page 73: youtube.com/watch?v=iaElPV0FWJ0

Page 75: youtube.com/watch?v=2TRkiQGbxC8

Page 79: youtube.com/watch?v=rmlg5QkusFQ

Page 81: eliwhitney.org/7/museum/eli-whitney/cotton-gin

Page 81: archives.gov/education/lessons/cotton-gin-patent

Page 81: jstor.org/stable/1832812?seq=1#page_scan_tab_contents

Page 87: youtube.com/watch?v=Wv7ffGUnB-I

Page 90: youtube.com/watch?v=jiRgdaknJCg

Page 109: youtube.com/watch?v=EZL6RGkPjws